THE WIZARDS

Aberavon Rugby
1876-2017

"I knew Annie Mort, from Taibach, who before a match at Aberavon would drop goals from around 40 yards with either foot to entertain the crowd. I also knew a scrum half – 'Jimmy-one-arm' - who had lost an arm in the First World War. Jim (Evans) played with murderous brilliance for Cwmavon for years. He was particularly adept at stopping a forward bursting from the line-out with a shattering iron-hard thrust from his stump as he pulled him on to it with the other arm.

"I would rather have played rugby for Wales than Hamlet at the Old Vic. To that town, Aberavon and its rugby team, I pledge my continuing allegiance, until death"

Richard Burton

This book may help explain why Burton – and others – have felt that way.

THE WIZARDS

Aberavon Rugby
1876-2017

HOWARD EVANS &
PHIL ATKINSON

St David's Press

Cardiff

Published in Wales by St. David's Press, an imprint of

Ashley Drake Publishing Ltd
PO Box 733
Cardiff
CF14 7ZY

www.st-davids-press.wales

First Impression – 2017

ISBN
978-1-902719-66-5

British Library Cataloguing-in-Publication Data.
A CIP catalogue for this book is available from the British Library.

Typeset by Replika Digital, India
Printed by Akcent Media, Czech Republic

CONTENTS

This book is dedicated to all the splendid Aberavon players and supporters through the years, but in particular to: Andrew John, Ian Moore, Chris O'Callaghan, Gareth Gange, Cliff David and Paul Williams.

Also to my wife Shirley, and my great friend Phil Atkinson.

ACKNOWLEDGEMENTS 1

The season 2016-17 was 'officially' the 140th anniversary of Aberavon RFC. Like so many clubs, its origins in 1876-77 are sketchy, to say the least: and, again in common with others, it did close down for a few of those early seasons'. However, there is no doubt about rugby having existed in Aberavon for 140 years and more.

There was rugby played in the fields around Aberavon when Afan was the name used, and Taibach and Cwmavon joined in. The year 1876 as a club starting point has been handed down from generation to generation; who is to say that they were wrong?

So with just a few smaller, previous efforts having been published by supporters of Aberavon, with Premiership rugby secured by the club for at least two more seasons and since I am now 76, the time appeared right to bring out a fuller history of the club. I sat down and started writing and was soon well over 100,000 words, but have now settled on this trimmed-down version!

Acknowledgements begin at the top with Andrew John, the Chairman of Aberavon RFC, a splendid man and a self-made success in business who has helped the club find the right road both on and off the field. Current coach Jason Hyatt, a former club player, has had success since rejoining the 'Wizards' and has a former club captain, Lyndon Lewis, as his backs coach.

My thanks go to everyone I have ever known since joining Aberavon, but mostly to my friend Paul Williams, the club's programme editor, who worked on the photographs and added notes on seasons long before I was at the club.

Also thanks to the excellent website controller Gareth Gange and skipper Ian Moore ('Buddha'), whose play and general attitude made me say I never wanted to watch rugby again when (or if) he ever retires. Ian's try against Carmarthen Quins – to avoid relegation – reduced me to tears: it came when my health was not great and raised myself and every watcher, friend and foe, to great emotion.

Chris O'Callaghan, a former player, Cambridge Blue, coach and friend, has always inspired me onwards with both my life and with this book. Life members Cliff David, Doctor Keith James and the late Dewi Bowen, secretary Steve Wharmby, statistician Colin Walters and my good friend Ken Whyte have all played vital parts.

In Steve Jones the club has the most loyal and unsung man: groundsman, team manager and so on. Chris Gittins, who I knew from great days at Bonymaen; coaches Kevin Hopkins, Simon King, Nicky Lloyd, Barry Maddocks, Mark Jones, Craig Warlow, etc., etc. – I thank them all.

David Beaton, Richard Hook, Dai Walters, John Nightingale, Keith, Jeff, Max, all the backroom staff; former stars such as Morton Howells, the late John Collins, Les Keen, Ray Giles and other great men such as Richard Morris, Jamie Davies and Mike 'Footy' Harris; the Hawkins and Breeze families – where do I stop?

I must also mention Darryl Thomas, whose career ended prematurely with knee problems, but now a groundsman, and also coach of Baglan RFC. Darryl was everything I wanted to be as a back-rower – brave and a great clubman. He and Darren Ryan (who, like me, is from the Docks area of Cardiff) has given everything for the club, as has Chris Davies, ex-Wales Under-20 and Sevens cap, former club captain and now a splendid Commercial Manager.

Aberavon RFC is a happy ship and the players are a close-knit band. I am from Cardiff, but was welcomed immediately by all and sundry. I truly thank them all.

Also, my gratitude to people such as Tony Lewis (Kenfig Hill), John Griffiths, Tim Auty and Rob Cole, along with the contribution of photographers David Morgan and Tony Staton.

Through the club I have discovered wonderful new lands (like Cwmllynfell, Waunarlwydd and Tonmawr!) though Taulupe 'Toby' Faletau (from the age of three, he tells me) and his father (Kuli) somehow beat me to the latter club.

David Evans from the *South Wales Evening Post* (now retired) and Phil Blanche from the *Western Mail* (now with the Press Association), gave me the chance to report on and fall in love with Aberavon.

A ton of thanks goes to publisher Ashley Drake and to my friend Phil Atkinson, who so splendidly put together my ramblings.

My thanks to them all and so many more, but mostly thanks to the Aberavon players and supporters. I have had a 'wizard' time!

HOWARD EVANS
Cardiff
July 2017

ACKNOWLEDGEMENTS 2

Even more so than with our pleasingly well-received previous publication on *The King's Cup 1919 – Rugby's First World Cup*, I have to emphasise that all the 'heavy lifting', the detailed player and game research for this later foray on the great Aberavon Club has been undertaken by the indefatigably enthusiastic and knowledgeable Howard Evans: well done, sir!

My role has been largely confined to background, linkage editing and the odd image: placing his efforts into a context and providing brief historical settings for his hard-won gems of statistics and reportage.

It is helpful and important to recall and record in these pages and elsewhere the ups and downs of clubs which have for so long been vital institutions and outlets for our communities. Whatever the odds, long may they - and those like Howard who chronicle them - flourish.

PHIL ATKINSON
Newport
July 2017

(Please note that throughout the book - TAG refers to the Talbot Athletic Ground; NZ is short for New Zealand and RL for rugby league)

PREFACE

I have thought for a long while that it would be right to mark the 140th Anniversary of Aberavon RFC with a book - and lo and behold, here it is. There have been a few smaller booklets and productions over the years, to mark significant milestones along the way, but never a 'real' book.

So when our great friend Howard Evans 'volunteered' to write it, the die was cast. In this busy modern era in which we live, there can be little doubt that if Howard had not put it all together, the project simply would not have 'passed go'. Ably assisted by his close friend and rugby historian Phil Atkinson and publisher Ashley Drake we have finally achieved our goal. A sincere thank you is the very least we can offer to these three great rugby men.

As chairman for nearly 20 years now, it is a huge honour for me to introduce this book about the club I have loved dearly ever since the early 60s, when I started watching the Wizards with my father. My first memories of the old place are of the ageless Cliff David, who was then treasurer, walking up and down in front of the stand asking people to move up closer as there were hundreds waiting to get in.

Sadly those days have passed and like every club in Wales our crowds have dwindled, but Aberavon RFC lives on and proudly holds its rightful place amongst the best in the semi-professional game in Wales.

So, I hope you enjoy reading the history of one of Welsh rugby's foremost clubs, one that has produced many internationals and one that is honoured to represent the town of Port Talbot and its people.

Many thanks to everyone who has contributed to Aberavon RFC over the years, in whatever capacity: supporters, players, staff and officials, you have all played a part in ensuring the well-being of this great old institution, a club of which I am immensely proud to be the Chairman.

Diolch! Thank you all!

ANDREW JOHN
Chairman, Aberavon RFC
August 2017

FOREWORD

Allan Martin used to live at the end of our road. I found his daughter standing in our kitchen once. The front door was open and I think she'd just wandered in to have a look. She was only little, and anyway it was fine because her dad played for the Wizards.

The earliest memory I have of watching them play is with my Grampa. Freezing cold and sitting in the stand (never did understand how that made any sense), listening to the glorious Mrs Mainwaring 'urging' on her Billy and his boys, and me trying to summon up the courage to pipe up and join in.

I'll never forget that first time I shouted out at an Aberavon game – the peculiar mixture of embarrassment and exhilaration I felt as I heard my thin little voice and totally nonsensical cry of encouragement (it was something to do with chess, for God's sake!) float off towards John Bevan near the scrum and get lost amongst the steam rising up off that muddy shove of Welsh masculinity.

I always used to gaze nervously and a little awestruck over at the older boys messing around by the metal railings behind the posts. Not a Grampa in sight! Surely 'the man' would come and tell them off – for swinging on the bars or not watching the game properly or just being young! But he never did.

Until one heart-racing day I found myself one of them. Me and four devilish friends all sitting on top of the barrier that old men in flat caps more usually stood behind to watch the game, putting all our teenage

Michael Sheen, a lifelong supporter of The Wizards

effort into keeping our freezing cold backsides balanced on the excruciatingly painful iron bar whilst looking like we hadn't a care in the world.

One of us – it wasn't me, I swear – started to lose the battle and began falling backwards. Instinctively, he tried to grab onto his mate next to him to steady himself who in turn did the same thing to his neighbour and within seconds the entire crowd got to watch four young lads do the most spectacular synchronized head-first backward dismount straight onto the concrete steps.

We got a cheer and a round of applause from the stands. I think the game even stopped for a brief second as Ray Giles and the other players tried to work out what the hell was going on. I eventually found less painful ways to get a crowd to react. But I swear it was the Wizards who started it all.

MICHAEL SHEEN
August 2017

1

1876-1900

Start, stop, restart, grow.....

Afan Football Club – the name referring to the older settlement of Aberavon, which was on the western side of the town – was formed in 1876, and the club's name changed several times before settling as *Aberavon Rugby Football Club*.

Though the club was not a founder member of the Welsh Rugby Union, rugby had begun in the fields around Aberavon before the Union's 1880 conception. In the 1870s, Mansel Tinplate Works was built and its proprietors – Colonel D.R. David, Sidney Byass and Richard Cook Jenkins – encouraged the local workers to form a team.

The first press mention of a game was against a Neath side on a boggy pitch called Lang's Field in the New Street area in 1876, when players from Aberavon, Cwmavon and Taibach combined, though most of the team were seemingly from Aberavon.

There was mention of good play by Betheul ('Beth') Heycock of Afan, father of the Taibach butcher, Phil Heycock. 'Beth' played for Taibach and Aberavon until 1891 and then served on the club committee until he died in 1913. He was a forebear of Llewellyn, later Lord, Heycock.

On November 17, 1877 after the first ever game played by Maesteg a report stated *"A spirited game was played under Rugby Union rules. It resulted in favour of Maesteg. Good service was given by Aberavon players W. David Jenkins, G. Formby, F. W. David and Dr. Jack H. Davies."*

Neath historian Mike Price records a game at Port Talbot Wharf in March 1878 between Neath and 'Cwmavon' which Neath won, as they did again a week later. He states that Aberavon played Neath Seconds until 1888-89, when regular first team fixtures between the sides began, while on October 31, 1878 there was a game against a team from Bridgend, with Afan winning by a goal and three tries at Port Talbot.

Both Formby and 'Beth' Heycock played for Neath against Swansea in Cup matches of 1877 and 1878, and in early March 1879, Aberavon beat Maesteg by three tries to nil with M.A. Jenkins as captain. On March 8,

Aberavon were due to host Cardiff, but it appears that Cardiff instead met Newport in a cup-tie: then, on March 24 Bridgend, at home, defeated Aberavon.

In those early days the headquarters were at a variety of fields – firstly, one below Jenkins Bros., on which New Street was later built. Next, around 1879, came Kent's Field (also called the Wharf Field), at the docks near the Tiddle Wink Tavern, which was bought by Lieutenant L.R. Fitzmaurice, a former harbourmaster who had two sons in the team. Temporary pitches were also used at the site of the subsequent Tydar Street.

These were in the docks area, and the old Mansel Cricket Field and Daycock's Field (with grandstand and changing rooms), were later developed and taken for the steelworks, so the club moved to a site leased from the Margam Estate and Captain Andrew Fletcher of Margam Castle. This was to become the Central Athletic Ground, gained with a loan coming from Sir Sidney Byass. (The club committee brought the pitch up to scratch and it was from then on their active home, with a hiatus in 1914 when the Government turned it into allotments for the war effort.)

Back in the 1870s and 1880s, though, dressing rooms were mostly at local inns, including the Victoria Packet, The Oddfellows, The Grand Hotel, The Eagle Temperance Hotel (on the site of the Margam Estate Office) and even the Public Baths. Teams met at Ye Olde Castle, originally the Castle Hotel, and later, the more luxurious Hong Kong Hotel.

In 1879 Aberavon lost at home to Llanelli in their first meeting, played at The Burrows in Port Talbot: the clubs met next in March 1889 at Llanelli and again in September 1892. In December 1879 Tondu were defeated by three goals and one try to nil.

The history of Porthcawl states that Aberavon failed to turn up in October 1880, so Porthcawl played their first-ever match against Bridgend. Aberavon, once more joined by players from Cwmavon and Taibach, lost by two dropped goals to nil against Neath, when the captain was M. Jones and Beth Heycock played for the 'Combined' team.

On Boxing Day 1881 Aberavon met Tondu with: Thomas Jones, W. Martin, Rees Edwards (Captain, and a singer who emigrated to the USA), Jack Mainwaring (of the Caradoc Inn, Sandfields), Will A. Jones, W. Hopkin Rees, W. Barrow, A. Johns, W. Wlliams, F. Jones, P. Jones, Richard (Dick) Thomas, D.J. Thomas, Thomas Davies and Alex David.

Cwmavon had formed their own team and played at Port Talbot Wharf in 1881, a year before Aberavon were to take part in the South Wales Challenge Cup – and lose at Swansea by 44-0 on February 4, 1882.

In that 1881-82 season Martin Jenkins was the first named secretary known, with Dr Jack H. Davies was captain. Jack was a hard man and had fought bare-knuckle on Aberavon Beach, hammering a professional boxer, Bill Samuel.

After the old Afan club had faded away Aberavon Red Rovers were formed, with workers from Byass & Co., but then in 1887 a public meeting re-established the town team, as the Red Rovers merged with players from Taibach and the Old College Boys.

Aberavon were then at the Mansel Works ground, with the first game, on October 18, 1887, being a 0-0 draw against Penygraig. The team included Dr. Davies as captain and Ivor Griffiths, formerly of Red Rovers. He then became captain for seven seasons and also a Wales reserve.

The side was: Rhys Lewis; Crane Alford, Evan Edwards, David H. James, R. (Dick) Henda; George Bowen, Jonathan Peters; Ivor Griffiths (capt), W. Jack Harries, 'Beth' Heycock, William J. (Bill) Wilkins, Joe ('Cilfrew') Hopkins, W. Hopkin Rees, Martin Rees and Billa Grace.

By 1888, too, the club was accepted into the Welsh Rugby Union and in November 1889 was also fielding a second team.

On January 22, 1890, Aberavon lost away to Cardiff Harlequins and fielded – Dick Hendra; Tom Shaw-Roberts, D. (or H) Thomas, David James, Evan Edwards; George Bowen, Jonathan Peters; Ivor Griffiths (capt), Jack Harries, Bill Wilkins, Crane Alford, 'Cilfrew' Hopkins, Sam Lewis, Tom Jones, Jack H. Davies.

The report of the match stated that: *"A ONE-ARMED MAN played well and gathered the ball better than his colleagues!!"* It proved to be the forward, William J. (Bill) Wilkins, who had indeed lost an arm. Clearly, Richard Burton was not the only local to have known of limbless wonders. The works, then the war, took their toll.

That year rugby grew strong in the Aberavon and Port Talbot area and Bridgend were thrashed, so

Aberavon in August 1888: Back row – Fred W. Butler (secretary/ treasurer), Tom Jones, Bill Wilkins, Tom Shaw-Roberts, Evan Edwards, Jack Harries, Dick Thomas, Dick Hendra, Humphrey Leyshon (asst secretary). Seated – Bill Clements, Sam Lewis, Ivor Griffiths (Capt), Billa Grace, Joe ('Cilfrew') Hopkins, George Bowen. Front – Rees Hopkins, Jonathan Peters.

it was maybe no surprise when, six months later, Bridgend failed to appear for a game at Aberavon.

Perhaps Aberavon should have followed suit on December 13, 1890 when, away to Llanelli Harriers, it was so cold that the game resembled 'touch rugby'. No 'collaring' was allowed, and if a player was touched a scrum was formed. Two weeks later, Bridgend captain E. Emery was bitten by a dog on the pitch and both player and dog left the field!

In 1891 came one of the roughest-ever clashes, as Aberavon won at Bridgend with one Bridgend and two Aberavon players sent off, while five days later Penygraig walked off at Aberavon after disagreeing with the home side's third try. Boxing Day, though, despite its name, proved rather less dramatic on all fronts, the Mayor of Aberavon kicking off against Pontefract in a 0-0 draw.

The club's standing began to be recognized, too, with representative honours for its players. In 1892 Ivor Griffiths and Jack Harries played for Glamorgan and both appeared in a Wales Trial along with J. Evans. Overall in 1891-92, Aberavon's record read: P 27, W 14, D 5, L 8.

The *Western Mail* recorded: *"If Aberavon had shown in the early part of the season anything like the form they exhibited during the last three months, their record would have been a brilliant one for a club in the third year of its (latest) existence. After commencing in good style, the team had the misfortune to lose the services of two trustworthy backs. From December, with Jonathan Peters recovered from his accident, victory succeeded victory, only interrupted by an occasional draw. From December 20 to April 15, 13 matches were played without defeat with 15 goals and 13 tries against one try."*

Aberavon went on to defeat Kent Wanderers 8-0, although Kent had included at least three 'guest' players, including the legendary W.J. ('Billy') Bancroft, and despite Aberavon being described as *'poorly represented'*. A try and conversion by Dick Hendra broke the deadlock.

Aberavon's team of 1890, captained by Ivor Griffiths.

In November, Penygraig 'A' walked off while losing away to Aberavon 'A' and then in the first-ever first-team game with Swansea, the 'All-Whites' were not keen to play their best side and only used a handful of regulars in the 0-0 draw. Ivor Griffiths captained Aberavon and the pack was said to be very strong, averaging 11st. 11lbs: heavy for those days!

Aberavon won seven and drew two, being unbeaten until the New Year when they fell 5-6 at home to Penarth. Then, for a match at Aberavon in February 1893, several Llandaff players waited for the 3.00pm train at Ely Station in west Cardiff, but said it did not stop: as a result they never arrived. March 11 brought the first-ever meeting with Cardiff's First XV, but Aberavon lost at the Arms Park by four tries, three conversions and a drop goal to nil.

Meanwhile Ivor Griffiths played for Glamorgan against Lancashire at Swansea, in the first-ever game played by an English County on a Welsh ground. Having played at Cardiff Harlequins, Aberavon then 'toured' the West Country, travelling to Devonport the following day, meeting Redruth two days later and then Torquay the day after: four matches in five days!

The Mayor (maybe not the same one) kicked off in a match between a combined 'Volunteers' and District of Aberavon XV against Glamorgan Police in aid of Port Talbot Intermediate School, with the Chief Constable of Glamorgan also present.

Many tinworkers had worn the red (or 'blood') and black and dockers were also to became a great force for the club before steelworkers took up their huge role. Numbers were swelled and in 1893 the Aberavon 'A' XV also had full fixtures, fielding strong men who found a real release from their hard and often dangerous manual work for 80 minutes on a rugby pitch.

Aberavon, too, grew stronger and the win at Llanelli in November 1893 was, according to Llanelli records, the first over them by Aberavon. A surprise, too: it caused the Llanelli secretary and former international, Harry Bowen, to state: *"We ought never to be beaten by Aberavon!"*

In January 1894, rugby continued despite a smallpox epidemic and in a defeat by 3-5 against Devonport Albion at Plymouth, the winning try came after a touch judge raised his flag only to be ignored by the referee. Aberavon appealed to the RFU, but the result stood.

One report of a home game against Bridgend said that Aberavon *"... kicked off at the Railway End"*. The railway station was at the bottom of Tanygroes Street (where Taibach play). This reference would have been before the Central Athletic Ground (later Talbot Athletic Ground) days, and the game was probably played on that Mansel Field, near the old Rhondda and Swansea Bay railway line: it also served the local sporting community as home to Port Talbot Cricket Club until the land was acquired for the site of the new hospital.

(Years later there was a 'railway end' at the TAG, as a line ran on an embankment around one whole end and side of the pitch, and crossed the road outside the ground where Sinclairs Garage now stands. The row of houses overlooking the ground behind the scoreboard is called Bridge Terrace, a reference to the old railway bridge there.

Before the M4 motorway was built, the line used to follow its present course, terminating at sidings in Dyffryn Yard to the north of Taibach, near the present Junction 40. The remains of the old embankment provide the covered enclosure behind the posts and the main terracing opposite the stand. The land was gifted to Aberavon when the line closed.)

On April 28, 1894, in the Aberavon and District Challenge Cup Final for a cup donated by David Jones of the Assembly Rooms, Aberavon 'A' beat Maesteg, as holders Briton Ferry refused to play.

The overall tally for 1893-94 read: P 34, W 18, D 9, L 7 and the AGM in September reported that the club's finances were also in credit, with a balance of £30. The President was Sidney Hutchinson Byass, Vice-President F.G. Jenkins, Secretary Fred W. Butler and Assistant Secretary Humphrey Leyshon, who gave over 20 years' service. It was proposed to build a grandstand – but only if Miss Talbot would grant a lease on the ground.

On the playing front, in October 1894 George Trick returned to Neath, while Ivor Griffiths 'retired', but returned a few weeks later. The season progressed well and Neath were met at the Bird in Hand Field, while against Penarth the referee pulled out. No problem – the two club secretaries took the whistle for a half apiece!

More county honours were recorded, Dan Jones and Charlie Bamsey playing for Glamorgan against Lancashire in 1895 before being joined by Griffiths against Devon, while Fred Butler and Bill Howells played in the return.

That same year saw a run of nine successive wins, and though Barnstaple failed to appear, Aberavon went to Barnstaple a month later, won, and two days later played at Devonport. Bedford were beaten 9-0 in January, and the clubs were not to meet again for 82 years!

In November 1895 the 0-0 draw with Pontypridd was refereed by their secretary, while in the same month the Mayor of Aberavon (who else?) kicked-off against Lampeter College. However, the ground was closed by the WRU for 24 days in 1896 after disorderly conduct – by the crowd – at home to Morriston. Aberavon then played five away games in eight days with four lost and one drawn, but the season ended with a win at Neath.

October 1896 saw Penygraig leave Aberavon after 15 minutes of heavy rain while they were losing. They did not return and the entrance money was refunded. Before the end of the year Aberavon won 12 of 16 games before losing at Penarth, while Griffiths and Dan Jones again played for Glamorgan.

In 1897 club member and Ireland hockey cap, Fred Butler, joined the WRU and in 1899 twins Lewis M. Thomas and William R. Thomas, MBE, were players with 'W.R.', despite having three years at Newport, being captain in 1907-08, and then chairman, life member from 1910 and WRU vice-president. Humphrey Leyshon became secretary with Tom Griffiths assistant and J. H. Grant as treasurer.

Humphrey Leyshon was also a WRU life vice-president and club president, while Sidney Byass, Aberavon's greatest benefactor, loaned the club £7,000. He was chairman of Glamorgan cricket, Mayor of both Aberavon and Port Talbot and was knighted in 1926, but he died on February 18, 1929 and when his son died in 1976, the Byass Baronetcy title became extinct.

In 1897 Aberavon had their first capped player when scrum half Dan Jones scored a debut try as England were beaten at Newport but he was never selected again. He considered moving to Rugby League (RL), only for Colonel David to persuade him otherwise.

Ivor Griffiths was a Wales reserve and Dan Jones was picked to play as a 'guest' with his Wales half-back partner Selwyn Biggs for Cardiff against Bristol, but it was called off due to frost, Further chances were restricted, as Scotland then refused to play Wales during the dispute which classed Arthur Gould of Newport a professional, and Ireland followed suit.

Stories familiar to most Welsh clubs pepper the press files: Llanelli cancelled a game because of too many injuries, while in April 1897 the train carrying the players to Torquay arrived 90 minutes late, but Aberavon still won. Two days later, 2,500 saw a draw at Barnstaple and on the next day an Evan Jones try at Devonport Albion took the spoils.

The season ended with a record of P 39, W 21, D 2, L 7, Neath being beaten 19-6 on May Day in a 'friendly', with receipts going to the unemployed, while October 1897 saw the WRU declare backs J. Jones and Rhys Lewis to be professionals (though Jones, the brother of Dan, was later let off.)

Aberavon started 1898-99 with what was considered their best-ever team and with Glamorgan policeman Alfred 'Bobby' Brice in the pack. Before the year's

Dan Jones, Aberavon's first cap.

Wales v England 1897: Arthur Gould (Newport) is the captain and scrum half Jones is in the centre of those in front.

turn came seven wins in eight games, the loss by 3-13 at Cardiff. Then, in January, Brice became Aberavon's second international and the first forward selected from the club. He also played for Somerset and Glamorgan County sides, and moved to the Arms Park club.

Dan Jones broke an ankle against Pontypridd with referee Wat Thomas, the old Neath player, being hit by a stone and threatened by Aberavon spectators. The ground was suspended by the WRU from March to November 1899 but on appeal the ban was ended in September though Thomas had reported acting captain Tim Madden for calling him a cheat and refusing to go off when dismissed.

Madden was suspended until the end of November and forward 'Billo' Thomas, who called on the crowd to hit the referee, was suspended until January 1900, while committee-man Evan Jones, who threatened the referee was suspended from any committee or from being a touch-judge until April 1900. The referee praised secretary Leyshon and Pontypridd forward W.E. Rees for seeing him to safety.

On calmer notes, Val 'Bookie' Jones played for Glamorgan and the season ended with 0-0 draws away to Penygraig and Bridgend. The club's

1899 AGM showed a year's deficit of £25. Sidney Byass was returned as President; Humphrey Leyshon as Secretary and J.H. Grant as Treasurer. New Vice-Presidents were Reverend J.B. Moore and Phil Roberts and the name of the club altered *to 'Aberavon and Port Talbot'*.

On December 23, skipper Dan Jones failed to appear at Bridgend and after 30 minutes, a forward, T. David (ex-London Welsh) came on with Lewis Thomas going to scrum half, but on Boxing Day, Dan was back to help beat Maesteg with Thomas scoring three tries from wing – the first hat-trick recorded by an Aberavon player.

The year ended with Aberavon unbeaten since November 4 at Swansea, though those 'All-Whites' called off fixtures after 'excessive rough play by Aberavon'. Behaviour was clearly a regular concern all round: the price of a Stand Season Ticket was then ten shillings, a Field Season Ticket five shillings, but a 'Special Notice' in the tickets read *"All persons found betting or swearing on the Ground will be prosecuted."*!

The club colours were originally white, but they later became scarlet and black hoops, then red and black hoops, in each case with navy blue knickers. One notable fact of this era was that as with many other clubs, despite good attendances, games regularly kicked off some 30-60 minutes late, particularly where a lot of travelling was required. In local reports of the time Bridgend were often tagged *'The Asylum Boys'*, while Aberavon were *'The Avonites'*.

Perhaps fittingly in the light of the 'almighty' derby rivalry that was to grow between the sides, when Aberavon met Neath at the Gnoll on February 10, 1900 they were refereed by a clergyman – the Rev. J.S. Longden! Only 13 days later came a huge blow, though, as skipper Dan Jones was forced to retire after suffering a further injury and Tim Madden took over as captain. As the millennium dawned, the club record for 1899 1900 was: P 32, W 18, D 4, L 10.

In August the AGM was held at the Old Vestry Rooms and presided over by solicitor E.T. Evans. Sidney Byass was re-elected as President with Vice-Presidents E.T. Evans and Dr. Hartland, Secretary Humphrey Leyshon and Auditors Lemuel Jones and David L. Ware.

The definitive kit by the turn of the century was featured on one of a small set of cards of top clubs drawn by Western Mail ace cartoonist J M Staniforth.

2

1900-1918

Victory in the Cup: then war breaks out.....

'**B**obby' Brice was captain for 1900-01 and in October Dan Jones returned, but on November 3 Dan was injured against Swansea and Ogley Harris came in. This was the end for Dan, but he had been a great servant of Aberavon.

Around that period came the debut of George Vickery, aged 21, then not-yet capped by England. He was a superb forward, whose son Walter was to gain a Wales cap, while playing for Aberavon. Another 1900 debutant was Tommy 'Wigan' Thomas, who joined from the local Seaside Stars club.

A fine 14-3 home win over Llanelli in December was thought one of the club's best. Tries came from skipper Brice, 'Billo' Thomas and Tom Upton, after Harris had opened the score with a superb drop goal.

Alfred Bailey 'Bobby' Brice.

Newspapers had never really liked the 'Avonites' and now the language of the Aberavon supporters was hailed as 'filthy and abominable', but onfield another good scrum half, John 'Bala' Jones, received a cap against England early in 1901. That year too, though, the club lost the excellent Val ('Bookie') Jones to Salford RL.

Brice retained the captaincy for 1901-02 and in April there was a tour to the West Country when Devonport Albion, Redruth and Barnstaple were all played. The skipper in 1902-03 was Tim Madden, who was said to be 'as Welsh as the coal he helped ship at the docks', but there was a touch of Irish in him also. He played for 23 seasons and Ireland wanted to cap him, while when the WRU weighed him before a Trial match, his fellow dockers slipped lead weights into his kit. However, he was never capped for either country.

In November 1902 the team travelled to the famous Queen's Club in London's Kensington area and defeated London Welsh by 12-3 with four tries. At the end of

FATHER...George Vickery played for Aberavon and England in 1905.

DAN JONES...was Aberavon's first Welsh international in 1897.

...AND SON: Walter Vickery played for Aberavon and Wales, 1938-39.

Three Aberavon greats.

August 1903, the fine centre Willie Thomas signed for Salford RL, where he played 501 times and became their chairman. From 1902-1904 Irish international wing Arthur Freear played for Aberavon. He had won his

Aberavon's team of 1902-03 captained by Tim Madden.

11

Bobby Brice's Welsh cap of 1904.

caps with Lansdowne and he became licensee of the Castle Hotel, but he later left to join Hull RL.

In 1903-04 the captaincy went to the mighty George Vickery and in 1904 Aberavon were credited in the newspapers with a 13-0 home win over Cardiff, who refused to show that in their records, claiming they did not lose to them until January 19, 1921, when Aberavon proceded to run up seven successive wins over the capital club. The last match of the season was an extra fixture played, according to Swansea, *"to aid the cash-strapped Aberavon club"*.

Though he appeared 204 times for Cardiff, gaining 11 Wales caps, during January 1904 Cardiff forward Billy Neill (born William O'Neil) played some games for Aberavon. These seemingly came because he was a friend of Brice, who moved to Cardiff but continued his run of 18 consecutive Welsh caps with his competitive fourteen stone frame.

Arguments arose as to whether Aberavon should again run a second team and indeed, in 1904-05 Aberavon Reserves were formed, captained by fine forward Will Gregory, while under Vickery's leadership the first team became Glamorgan League Champions. Their season included a win over West Hartlepool just two days after Christmas and ended in style with a home success over Bristol.

Full back Tom Thomas took over as captain for 1905-06 and then Will Gregory in 1906-07, even though Thomas was pictured as the captain during that season, but the picture, including a player named as the Reverend T. Williams, may not have been the Aberavon First XV. In any event, Thomas turned to Wigan RL in December 1906.

By 1907-08 Aberavon had moved to their present location, which was at that time named the Central Athletic Ground. Their headquarters were at the Public Baths, while the ground was shared with soccer, tennis, hockey, running and quoits. On one occasion a 3-horse race over a mile (four times around the track) was staged, while spectators were entertained by the Aberavon Quoits Club, captained by champion thrower, Roger Hill.

Among the team who went to Glyncorrwg to open that new ground were Will James (later London Welsh captain, who then played in South Africa); Will's brother Arthur James (a building contractor from Eagle Street); Gwyn Jones (from the Angel Hotel on the old Causeway and a farmer at

Aberavon 1905-06, captained by Tom Thomas.

Tynewydd Farm, Baglan) and D.A. Davies (a printer and member of Wern Congregational Church).

Will Jones was the 1907-08 captain, but it was a poor season and included a crushing 0-19 loss away to Plymouth Albion. The 1908-09 season, under skipper Willie R. Thomas, began with a home loss to Cardiff, who stated it was a 'practice match', then on October 15 the club combined with Neath at the Gnoll against the first-ever 'Wallabies' touring side.

The game kicked off at 4.00pm so that local miners and children could attend, though Australia did not arrive by train until 90 minutes before the kick-off. Australia won 15-0, but their players and the referee had to be escorted off in disgraceful crowd scenes. Combined team captain D.H. Davies (Neath) had to leave with cracked ribs after 20 minutes play.

It caused the Australian forward Tom Richards, later in the British team to South Africa and awarded a Military Cross in the war, to state: *"Even if they had been winning, the crowd would have continued complaining and hooting."* Despite all that, Australian captain Dr 'Paddy' Moran, who scored the opening try, presented Thomas with his tour jersey.

In January, Arthur James was sent off in a 0-9 loss at Pontardawe, but in April Aberavon set off – to Ireland, apparently kissed the 'Blarney Stone'

On tour in Cork, Ireland 1909. Willie R. Thomas with the ball.

Neath/Aberavon v Australia 1908 - The programme

and then on the 13th defeated Cork. At least three ladies and about fifteen committee and supporters joined 19 or so players to make the trip. The season ended with a record of P 29, W 11, D 6, L 12.

By September 1909 the sharing of the Ground had caused many difficulties and the Committee resolved, apparently successfully, *"that an application be made to the Central Athletic Ground Committee asking for terms as sole tenants for exclusive rights of Rugby Football for next season. And that our groundsman be paid three shillings per match; gatemen two shillings and ticket sellers one shilling."*

Less successfully, it was during that 1909-10 season that Neath recorded four wins over Aberavon for the first time: and Llanelli also won four meetings. The club captain was the virtually unknown E. Pugh, while it was in January, 1910 that a knee injury ended the career of Willie R. Thomas and the game at

Pontypool had to be abandoned without a score after only 25 minutes, due to heavy rain.

In 1910-11 the powerful Rees Richards took over as captain, but it was not a great season, partly because of the many other local clubs now in existence. A church side, Aberavon St. Mary's, were undefeated Port Talbot League champions in 1909-10 (W 20, D 4). Among the others in the League were Cwmavon, Taibach and the church teams of St. Theodore's, St. Agnes and St. Paul's.

In February 1911 the committee resolved: *"that the Secretary speak to the forwards on the advisability of standing down in rotation, so that we may keep 10 forwards in good condition",* while after losing at home to Neath in April the committee added: *"that the Secretary must see the forwards and impress upon them the need of every man to scrummage and that the backs be asked to let the ball go and give it more air than it has previously received."*

The team bounced back, and after winning at Pontypool they recorded an outstanding 12-4 victory at Gloucester and scored two tries. Aberavon also celebrated the capping of their talented centre William Avon Davies against Scotland and Ireland. However, he was to join Leeds RL in 1913.

Ewan Davies played in the threequarters and gained two Wales caps in 1912 while playing for Cardiff. William George Evans, a 1911 Wales cap gained with Brynmawr, was in the pack, but transferred to Leeds RL, later returning to live in Port Talbot and die there in 1946.

Jimmy Donovan, who worked in the light plate mill of the old steelworks, was the captain in 1911-12 when a game at Pontypool in March was called off as Aberavon were held up in traffic and arrived too late to play, there being no floodlights. The game was replayed two days later with Pontypool winning. There were wins over Neath by 4-0 in October and 3-0 away in March, while the season's record was: P 32, W 20, D 6, L 6.

In season 1912-13 the South Africans arrived and Will Hopkins (later Aberavon skipper) faced the tourists in the Glamorgan side beaten by 3-35 at Cardiff on October 17. Five days earlier, Llanelli had defeated Aberavon, though Aberavon walked off in protest as the referee did not appear and Ewart Hughes from Llanelli had taken over.

William Avon Davies: Wales 1912.

Aberavon were not pleased with his decisions, but after a while returned to play on.

Fiery Rees Richards returned as captain and in December local police were engaged by Aberavon to take tickets at the gates, which posed the question as to the honesty of the gatemen (or the strength of those attempting to enter without paying?) Entry to the field was three pence.

In April the death occurred of Ivor Griffiths, who was skipper for eight seasons. Aged 41, he died in Boulder, Western Australia, where he had gone to live and work. Skipper Richards had played in Welsh wins against Scotland, France and Ireland, but later that year he, too, 'went north', joining Wigan RL. The overall record was: P 32, W 19, D 8, L 5.

A Port Talbot School pupil, Theodore Guthrie Morgan of Tŷ'r Eglwys in Cwmavon, who attended Llandovery College and played for London Welsh, gained entry to Keble College, though he just failed to win a Blue for Oxford at fly half. His brother, Stewart, was also at Oxford.

Next came an important milestone as on July 26, 1913 Miss Emily Charlotte Talbot granted exclusive use of the Central Athletic Ground to Aberavon, with the Club was granted a lease of 39 years at nominal rent. It was, in recognition, called The Talbot Athletic Ground (TAG): and so it still is.

During 1913 a Taibach bantamweight named Billy Beynon was British boxing champion and when Aberavon were short against Pontypool, Billy, who had played for St. Theodore's Juniors, donned the jersey, which went down to his knees. Undaunted, he played without shorts! He died in a colliery accident in 1932, aged 42.

The strong Will Hopkins was captain for what proved a memorable 1913-14 campaign, which yielded final figures of P 38, W 25, D 7, L 6. Tom Ponsford played for Somerset and in February Jonny Davies left, with two friends, to live in Pittsburgh, USA.

Cardiff and Newport had announced that they would not give Aberavon fixtures that season and were attacked by international Willie Trew, who said: *"Aberavon are without question one of the best teams playing this Rugby game. I cannot understand what the two clubs are thinking about as it does Welsh Rugby no good."*

In that season the pack included the Reverend Austin Davies, a curate of St. Theodore's. Whether through divine intervention or that fierce eight, the side had a splendid run before the eventful new year of 1914, though the 8-8 draw with Llwynypia saw three sent off, including Aberavon forward John Atkinson. As sometimes occurs, they then all left the field together *'laughing and joking'*, with no ill-feeling.

Aberavon did not lose from September 20 until February 28, when they fell at Pontypool. A week earlier they had beaten Llanelli 6-0 in ankle-deep mud as 'Warhorse' Jones and 'Pandy' Rees scored tries.

In the Challenge Cup, Aberavon beat Swansea on April 2 with Dai Griffiths at full back and in five days (April 10-14) they won four away games – at Bridgwater, Devonport Albion, Newton Abbot and Bristol.

At home, Neath were beaten with Aberavon having Swansea's Billy Bancroft 'guesting' and dropping a goal in the 7-0 scoreline. On April 20 came the Cup quarter-final at Glanamman, as Amman Utd were beaten 3-0 by a Charlie Jones try: the referee was famous former Welsh half back Willie Trew.

Aberavon won 9-0 at Bridgend in the last non-cup game of the season, which saw Wales fly half Clem Lewis brought into the home side. Aberavon centre Guthrie Morgan landed a goal from a mark and scored a try, while the final touchdown came from the speedy forward Tom Ponsford, who played the whole match on the wing. Before war broke out, both he and 'Warhorse' Jones were to be selected by Glamorgan against Monmouthshire.

Welsh Challenge Cup winners 1913-14
Inset: J. Davies. T. Guthrie Morgan,
Top Row: O. Harris (trainer), D. Randell, Jim Jones, Bob Randell, D. Tobin, T. Ponsford, D. Rees, Charlie Jones, J. Atkinson, Buller Jones.
Second Row: D.W. Jones (Hon. Treasurer), Ivor Hopkins, E.B. Rees, H. Leyshon (Hon. Secretary), W. Hopkins (Capt.), L.M. Thomas (Chairman), A. Waters, W.J. 'Pandy' Rees.
Bottom Row: Fred Potter, Con Evans, I. Harris, W. Jones (vice-capt.).

ABERAVON WIN THE CUP:

The South Wales Challenge Cup had begun in 1877-78 and ran until 1886-87, faltered, then restarted two years later and continued until 1896-97. It was revived in 1901-02 for three seasons and called the South Wales Junior Cup. Then, a decade on, in the 1913-14 season it was to make its last appearance until 1971-72. Back then, though, 42 clubs took part, split into Eastern and Western areas.

Llanelli had been disqualified, as the WRU suspended the amateur status of the Rev W. T. Havard (though he was to go on to win a cap in 1919), while Blaina surprisingly won a tough semi-final over Llwynypia, 3-0.

May 2, 1914 was to prove an historic day, then, with Aberavon winning the South Wales Challenge Cup at Bridgend by defeating Blaina 10-0 before a crowd of some 6,000. The game began at 5.15pm with well over 1,000 having travelled in trains and brakes from the Afan area, and the match was contested with fine vigour and dash, but in the very best sportsmanlike spirit.

An even tussle saw the first half end 0-0, but then, favoured by a stiff wind, Aberavon asserted themselves and after a brilliant burst by Ponsford, playing as 'rover', play was carried to the Blaina line and Fred Potter burst over from close range and converted. Smart Aberavon forward work set up another attack and again Potter scored and converted, before Guthrie Morgan missed a drop shot by inches.

The crowd assembled around the grandstand and amidst frantic cheering, Jim Jarrett, a Monmouthshire WRU member, presented the cup to skipper and hooker Will Hopkins, who, with others, was carried shoulder high. When they arrived home there was another huge crowd to give them a reception and a band led them through the streets. Gate receipts at the match were £155.

Aberavon were strong up front even though Bob Randall and Jim Jones had not yet been capped; the fair-haired 17-yrs-old Cwmavon-born Evan B.Rees at centre gained his only cap against the NZ Army while with Swansea in 1919. Ponsford, employed by Port Talbot Borough Council for many years, was said to have had an outsanding game.

Eight months after his cap, Rees joined Dewsbury RL and served in the South Wales Borderers during WWar1. The pack included Dan Tobin, Dai Rees, John Atkinson (from Porthcawl) and 'Warhorse' Jones, who had been a Wales reserve and was to lose an arm in the war.

Vice-captain Willie Jones partnered Potter at half back, but a late change at full back saw the stockily-built William J. ('Pandy') Rees from Cwmavon come in as Ike Harris was forced to drop out and the original choice, D. Griffiths, was ineligible. 'Pandy' was a local schoolteacher and had represented Glamorgan, later being Aberavon secretary.

Another late change saw right wing Ivor Hopkins (who lived until 90) drop out and Constable Hurford come in while Alf Waters appeared on the left wing for the final. Little Con Evans was the normal scrum half, but he missed out along with E.J. ('Buller') Jones and David Randall (brother of Bob).

The trainer was Ogley Harris, Ike's brother and a former fly half, while Lewis Thomas was club chairman; Humphrey Leyshon secretary and D.W. Jones the treasurer. It was said that every Aberavon player who had helped win the Championship and the Cup was presented with a gold 'Albert' watch chain.

Fly half Fred Potter, then, had notched all the points and though he was later reported to have gone to Cardiff, they have no record of him. The war was to spoil many a fine rugby Career: and much more, and more serious, besides.....

The Cup-winning team was: William J. ('Pandy') Rees; A. Hurford, Theodore Guthrie Morgan, Evan B. Rees, Alf H. Waters; Fred Potter, Willie Jones; Will Hopkins (capt), Dan Tobin, John Atkinson, Charlie ('Warhorse') Jones, Dai Rees, Jim Jones, Tom Ponsford and Bob Randall. The referee was Tom Schofield of Bridgend.

Former Cardiff and Wales cap W.M. Douglas said: *"I was surprised by this good Football game. It shows that the old Cup would still do much more for the good game of Rugby."*

When Dan Tobin died in 1980 aged 91, the great Miah McGrath said: *"Dan was an outstanding player who played up front in the pack in the days before the emergence of a specialist hooker. He was the last of the 1914 Cup team to die. He was a huge man, who was a foreman rollerman in the Bull Ring at the Mansel Tinplate Works, where men had to be tough to exist."*

The Cup was not played for again until 1971-72, though it seems that the cup that Aberavon won was used in the 1970s for the National Sevens and then went missing!

RUGBY 1914-1918: SOME WARTIME SNIPPETS

Σ Upon the outbreak of War the club committee resolved that no football should be played during hostilities and hoped *"that all young men, instead of filling up their time playing football during the winter, will consider the appeal made by Lord Kitchener to fill the ranks and thereby assist to save this country from the hands of the enemy."*

Σ The ground was used as allotments as Britain 'dug for victory' and the clubhouse has a plaque to 2nd Lieut. Rupert Price Hallowes, VC, MC, who was killed at Hooge, Belgium in 1915, being in the Artist's Rifles, Fourth Battalion Middlesex Regiment (Duke of Cambridge's Own). He was an assistant manager of the Mansel Tinplate works, and there is a memorial to him in the Neath & Port Talbot Hospital.

Σ The *Cambria Daily Leader* of April 24, 1914 reported that Mr Llewelyn George, recently of the Port Talbot Hotel, Aberavon, but now of 87, Lappin Avenue, Toronto, Canada, said that he and others have been instrumental in forming a British Rugby Football Union in Toronto, and up to date were are ten clubs affiliated of various nationalities, English, Irish, Scotch, American, Overseas and Welsh. Mr. George is the secretary for the Welsh clubs and representative for the League and at the last meeting of the league it was decided to write to the various 'old country' newspapers to the effect that the new Union would be pleased to hear of any football player who intended emigrating to Canada, so that the Union could assist him in securing a job. Mr. George said that the game had taken on well and several substantial people had already provided financial assistance.

Σ In 1914 Lieut. Bernard Oppenheim, a Rifleman with the King's Rifle Corps, who had played for Aberavon, was severely wounded: he died on 30th November 1917. Fred Richards, of Aberavon, Bridgend, Glamorgan Police and Whitchurch, was killed in action in 1915. Sgt. D. Thomas (Penarth/Aberavon) was killed in 1916 and wing Syd Thompson lost a leg. No doubt others fell, but records are unclear.

Σ Lieut. Theodore Guthrie Morgan was awarded the MC for bravery with the Salonika Forces. A captain in the 3rd Welsh Regiment, he later became rugby master at Dover College and had Wales full back Viv Jenkins on his staff. Morgan was later bursar and warden at the Imperial Service College, Windsor.

Σ Charlie ('Warhorse') Jones had an arm amputated at Norwich Hospital in 1916. In that year he had played for North Wales (Pals) Battalion and the 13th Royal Welsh Fusiliers. Dan Tobin played in October 1914 at Brighton for 'Wales' against 'England': all the players were recruits at the Shoreham Army Camp.

Σ Another to lose an arm was 20-yrs-old Jim Evans of Cwmavon, who played occasionally for Aberavon and Neath. Jim 'One-Arm' was that favourite quoted from Richard Burton's youth, having had his right arm blown off on the last day of war in 1918 and recuperated at Roehampton Hospital, where 'Warhorse' Jones was also resting. Jim had won 65 fights and later formed and captained Cwmavon Stars. In 1913 he had led Wales Schools against England, though he was working in Cynon Colliery. He joined the 5th Division in France and despite that one arm, played on for Cwmavon and became an Aberavon committeeman in the 1960s.

Σ The Cup final was the last official game that Aberavon played for just over five years, but there were charity games beginning on Christmas Day 1915 when Willie Trew's Swansea XV played a Will Hopkins' Aberavon XV with Trew as referee. Aberavon won with a try by scrum half Private Con Evans of the Bantam Battalion and the Aberavon Mayor, Councillor Percy Jacobs, kicked off with tea served afterwards at the Walnut Tree Hotel.

Σ In 1916 Evan B. Rees's XV beat E. ('Ned') Owen's XV 17-3, with gate receipts going to aid wounded Cwmavon soldiers and a Walter Rees (WRU Secretary's) XV met a Welsh Regiment XV with the Lady Mayoress kicking-off (made a change!).

Σ Aberavon beat a Maesteg XV and on Christmas Day 1916 the Third Welsh Ambulance Brigade defeated Aberavon 12-5.

Σ In August 1917 'Billo' Thomas was praised by a magistrate after knocking out a Russian seaman who had wounded a lady with a knife in Mabel Street, Port Talbot.

3
1919-1929

With the greatest era of 'the Wizards'.....

With the coming of victory and the peace treaties in 1918-19, rugby proper was to resume in Aberavon as elsewhere, if not as yet on the Athletic Ground. If these decades before 1939 – between the 'war to end all wars' and the next one – were not the easiest economically or socially for South Wales and other industrial heartlands of Britain, nor for much of Welsh rugby at grassroots or at international level, Aberavon managed to buck the trend successfully enough for several stretches of great achievement during those years.

Their rugby restarted on October 4, 1919 with a 4-0 (those dropped goals!) reverse at Maesteg but a week later Bryncethin were defeated at

Aberavon 1919-20 plus a Teddy Bear! The captain is Will Hopkins.

home – their temporary home, the Mansel Cricket Ground. The Management Committee met at the Victoria Institute, before moving to the TAG. (AGMs were held at the Constitutional Club, the Masonic Hall and, from 1968, at the Clubhouse.)

A team photograph for 1919-20 survives, taken outside the Vivian Hotel where the team changed for that nearby venue. It features a Teddy Bear mascot and Billie Bowen in his Navy uniform, while another from the same year has a grander background and in this one, Jim Jones has donned his Welsh jersey.

Flanker Jim had got the first of his six caps when Wales played the New Zealand Army side at Swansea in April 1919, and Will Hopkins, Aberavon's

SEASON: 1919/20.

ack Row.—D. W. Jones (Hon. Treas.), G. Mears, W. J. Thomas, Tom Ponsford (Vice-Capt.), D. Rees, J. Jones, D. Tobin, R. Randall, T. Parker, W. J. Rees (Hon.

2nd Row.—H. Leyshon (Hon. Sec.), J. Ring, D. H. Davies, W. Hopkins (Capt.), D. Jenkins, D. J. Hopkins, O. Harris (Trainer.)

Bottom Row.—W. J. Hopkins, R. Mitchell, Con Evans.

Aberavon RFC 1919-20

captain for 1919-20 (and 1920-21) had available a solid nucleus of fine experienced players from before the war, as well as promising others.

It was their quality and success that inspired a local bard, Owen ap Japheth (alias Thomas Owen David), to compose an Aberavon song entitled 'Bravon, Bravon.' To the tune of 'My Bonnie lies over the Ocean', it gave a mention to many players with these words: –

> 'Bravon, oh Bravon, you've got to beat (opposition's name) today.
> There's Ring, Dai 'Hunt' Davies, Bob Randall and Mears, Tom Ponsford, Jim Jones and old Dan (Tobin).
> They pass and repass the old leather together, each one knows how to tackle his man.
> There's Parker and Rowlands the boys from the Cwm, Will Hopkins, Con Evans and Ould,
> There's W. J. Thomas, Willie Hopkins half-back and a full back most daring and bold.'

That full back was David (Dai) Williams, formerly of Swansea, while another verse included: 'It takes a good wing to beat Johnny Ring, and the full back you can't beat at all.'

Another full back, former Wales cap and 1938 GB tourist, Vivian Jenkins, wrote in his Sunday Times column in 1976: "It was sometime in the winter of 1920-21 that I first caught sight of Aberavon, playing at the Old Mansel Field, now Sandfields. I was one of a group of small boys who crawled through a gap in a corrugated fence to get a free view of the men soon to become my heroes.

"Legendary wing Johnny Ring was the talk of the town and he seemed the fastest thing on two legs. Fast he must have been, because he was the highest try-scorer in the club history and I was thrilled when he was capped at Twickenham in 1921. Wales lost, but Johnny scored a try. It broke my heart when he went to Rugby League and I shed tears of despair. For me Johnny is still the Bravon Boy that I used to sing about in the old war song."

Jenkins admitted he began senior rugby with Bridgend, but did play once for Aberavon, 'guesting' against Neath, and he lived to tell the tale!

"The best part of it to me was appearing in the red and black jersey at last. I had to wait a long time. A globe-trotting correspondent does not put down many roots, but mine, if anywhere, must be in Aberavon. I was born there in a little house on the top end of Pentyla Hill. One of my first schoolmasters at the Old Mountain School was Thomas Davie Griffiths, who ran the club as honorary secretary for over 20 years. One of my first playmates in Springfield and Seaview Terrace was Hywel Thomas, later the WRU president."

That new wing, Johnny Ring, was quickly noted as both a flier and a fine footballer, with good hands and a startling change of pace. He bagged 38 tries in 1919-20, while on February 28, 1920, 20-year-old Charlie Rowlands, a pre-war Wales under-15 cap who would get his senior cap in 1926, made a sensational debut with a try hat-trick in a win at Penarth.

Three wins over Neath and a 3-0 victory over Llanelli (played at Neath) helped mean an end-of-season total of: P 37, W 25, D 6, L 6, and Aberavon were on the verge of a golden era, the finest in the club's history.

In November 1920 *'A Record Crowd'* saw Neath beaten and against Penarth, it was Johnny Ring's turn for the try hat-trick while the fair-haired, jinking sidestepper Rowlands notched two. Then, in January, ten days after his Welsh trial, Ring was capped against England

Johnny Ring.

Aberavon XV v Neath, December 3rd 1921, the opening of the Central Athletic Ground
Back row: W.J. Ould, J. Jeremy, G. Bamsey. Second row (standing): H. Leyshorn, O. Harris, G. Mears, J.H. Davies, W.J. 'Noisy' Thomas, Bob Randell, D. Hunt Davies, Tom Ponsford, G. Reed, H.M. Fuller (Ammanford). Third row (seated): Dai Williams, T. Collins, Mr. S.H. Byass, Jim Jones (capt.), Mr. Horace Lyne (president, Welsh Rugby Union), C.F. Rowlands, T. Parker, Johnny Ring. Bottom row: Willie Jones, W.J. Hopkins.

Mr. Humphrey Leyshon
Sometime Hon. Secretary
Aberavon R.F.C.
Life Vice-President
Welsh Rugby Union

Mr. W. R. Thomas, M.B.E., J.P.
Sometime Chairman
Aberavon R.F.C.
President, Welsh Rugby Union
1954 - 55

Sir Sidney Hutchinson Byass, Bart.
Sometime President
Aberavon R.F.C.

Great men off the pitch.

at Twickenham. Wales lost, 17-3: and although Ring's try provided his side's only points, he was dropped!

Being on strike from his job, Johnny was about to join Maesteg, who had offered him a job, but Aberavon gave him work on the construction of the ground. Ever vigilant (or when it suited!) the WRU asked him if he was earning money for playing. However, they accepted his explanation that his work was with the contractor, nothing to do with Aberavon, and he went on to tally 41 tries in that 1920-21 campaign. The 'Ring' of truth, evidently!

The club's tally was P 40, W 28, D 5, L 7, including a double over Cardiff, while sadder news was the early passing of Lewis M. Thomas, a club chair, solicitor, coroner and WRU vice-president, who died in January 1921, aged just 44.

The mighty Jim Jones became captain in 1921-22 and December 3 saw the official opening of the Central Athletic Ground and new grandstand. Local contracting firm Andrew Scott had laid and fenced off the ground: half a century on, they were to rebuild the North Stand and help redevelop the National Ground at Cardiff Arms Park.

The opening was performed by backer and patron Sir Sidney Byass and WRU President Horace Lyne, before an 8-3 win over Neath. Scott's workforce had included the outstanding forward Tom Ponsford, who helped transform the surface after its wartime use as allotments.

He was now groundsman and 'unofficial' coach, with some surprisingly modern and effective methods, while further off the field, secretary 'Pandy' Rees and chairman Gwyn Cound were succeeded by Thomas Davie Griffiths and Willie Thomas respectively, with D. W. Jones as treasurer.

The fixture lists were increasingly impressive: at Leicester some 14,000 saw the 'Tigers' win 19-6 and on Christmas Eve Aberavon won 6-3 at Cardiff, returning to beat London Irish on Christmas Day.

Recruitment was not one-way, though: during 1921 Aberavon lost Bill Ould, a collier and a forward from Glyncorrwg, when he joined Glamorgan Police and played for Cardiff, being capped twice in 1924. Another forward, Charles Henry Pugh, educated at Port Talbot County School, switched to Neath, winning seven caps in 1924 and 1925 whilst in the Police.

There was no holiday for the home players on Easter Monday 1922: Aberavon played home twice! After fixture confusion it was resolved to turn out against Exeter in the morning and, 'after a light lunch', Guy's Hospital in the afternoon: the hosts won both in style.

Jim Jones, Wales 1919-1921.

They also defeated Northampton, while another of those Charlie Rowlands hat-tricks saw off Swansea, with further touchdowns by 'Hunt' Davies and Johnny Ring, and the season finished: P 46, W 33, D 2, L 11.

Ring, who is reputed to have scored seven tries in a game – which match is unknown – joined Wigan RL in August, after scoring 46 tries – and 125 overall in three seasons, to set an impressive record.

Jim Jones was again captain for 1922-23 and Aberavon won at home to Neath, away to Cardiff and home to Swansea, but four days after that latter victory, Gwyn Parker joined Wigan RL. The depredations of the Northern scouts, attracted by the quality, reputation and financial vulnerability of the South Welsh player – including many of Aberavon's – were always a danger.

The Times newspaper heralded a fine Aberavon effort away to the powerful Guy's Hospital, though a few regular players could not travel for a 3-3 draw, with acting captain Rob Randall's try against a Guy's penalty.

The club's enhanced standing was reflected in the growing number of Wales call-ups, as forwards Llew Jenkins (twice) and John H. Davies gained their caps, though the fears about travelling to Ireland during the troubles, the vagaries of selection under the system prevailing at the time, and the comparative paucity of Welsh wins meant there were not many – from any clubs – who got an extended run.

Aberavon won at Cardiff, thrashed Bath 26-3 with six tries and also won at Llanelli for a season's record reading: P 46, W 28, D 2, L 16. Younger readers may marvel at the number of games regularly played in a

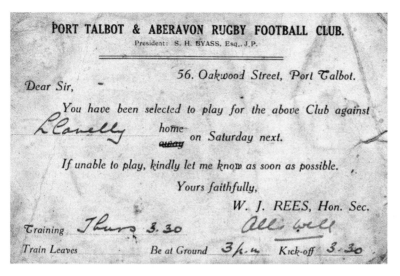

PORT TALBOT & ABERAVON RUGBY FOOTBALL CLUB.

President: S. H. BYASS, Esq., J.P.

56. Oakwood Street, Port Talbot.

Dear Sir,

You have been selected to play for the above Club against *Llanelly* home ~~away~~ on Saturday next.

If unable to play, kindly let me know as soon as possible.

Yours faithfully,

W. J. REES, Hon. Sec.

Training *Thurs 3.30*   *All well*

Train Leaves   Be at Ground *3 p.m.* Kick-off *3.30*

Aberavon selection card.

campaign, let alone representative and international calls. This was so right up to the 1980s, in the heyday of club rugby.

Now dawned what were to be those golden years for the club, as a fine start to 1923-24 saw nine wins. From December 1922 until Boxing Day 1923 they were unbeaten at home, with a powerful pack including skipper Rob Randall, Brin Phillips, Llew Jenkins, John Davies and John Stanley Davies.

By the year's turn the Red and Blacks were rated alongside Cardiff as the strongest club sides in Wales, and an 8-4 win over the Blue and Blacks saw wings Evan Williams and Will James cross for tries and Jack Jeremy convert one. The team was: G. Williams; Will H. James, D.'Hunt' Davies, Charlie Rowlands, Evan Williams; Willie J. Hopkins, J Thomas; Rob Randall (capt), Jack Jeremy, Brin Phillips, W. J. ('Noisy') Thomas, E. J. Stanley Davies, P.C. Tom Bennett, P. R. Vaughan and Llew Jenkins.

In 1924 Brin Phillips, who was capped against England, landed a goal from a mark in the club's win at Swansea. Randall, aged 33, was also capped, against Ireland in a game watched by the Duke of York and the first Labour Prime Minister, Aberavon M.P., Ramsay MacDonald. Randall gained a further cap against France.

In February, when Aberavon held off Neath 6-3 at the Central Athletic Ground the attendance exceeded all expectations as a Jeremy penalty and Rowlands try sealed victory. It was said that the threequarters – Will James, Dai 'Hunt' Davies, Evan Williams and Charlie Rowlands – were outstanding and Aberavon took the Championship – a feat that they were to repeat for the next three seasons.

Clearly great team spirit – as both cause and effect – came into play, and the side often met up at a cobbler's shop near Parry's Corner in Ysguthan Road, Aberavon for tactics and banter. Once, Llew Jenkins memorably

The Wizards of the West.

turned up on a horse and wearing the plus-four trousers of the fashionable golfer! It was certainly an above-par season for the club, with a final tally of P 42, W 33, D 4, L 5.

The South Wales Evening Post reporter, Bill Taylor ('Rover'), dubbed Aberavon the 'Wizards of the West' at this stage, and the name 'Wizards' was to stick. Indeed, the club emblem became a Wizard in the late 1940s and remains so to this day.

'Noisy' Thomas was captain in 1924-25 and in November's huge clash, Aberavon won 10-9 at Newport in their first-ever win there. Llew Jenkins scored a try that 'Hunt' Davies converted and scrum half Shon Thomas fooled the great Jack Wetter to score the winning try, while a victory at Guy's Hospital in December was hailed by *The Times* as *'Match of the Day in Britain'* and the opening half of the season saw just one defeat, 3-6 at Cross Keys.

Aberavon had nine Welsh caps in their squad around this era – until Rugby League scouts lured many of them away – and in January, 18-yr-old centre Evan Williams (an under-15 cap) joined Phillips, James and Hopkins in the Wales team against England. Evan had a fine game and all four played again against Scotland, but only Phillips was retained against Ireland and France. As a result, James and Williams turned to Rugby League later in the year.

The Wizards scored 12 tries in a 40-9 win at Bath, with Rowlands scoring either five or six depending on reports, and their second victorious unofficial

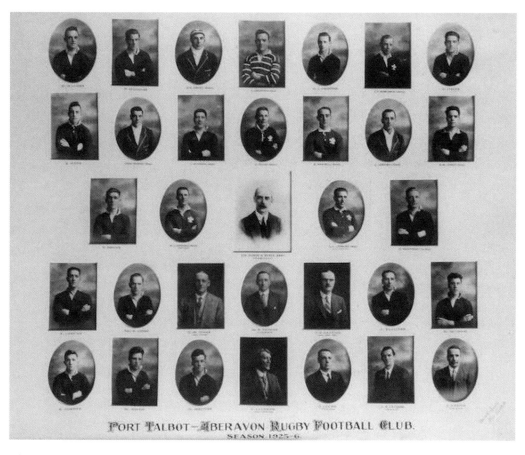

Aberavon 1925-26.

championship campaign ended P 42, W 31, D 4, L 6. A third successive Championship loomed in 1925-26 with Willie J. Hopkins as captain and despite Llew Jenkins taking up a job in Coventry in the New Year: he was to die there in 1973.

Jenkins, a Senghenydd collier who had joined the police in 1921, had 18 games for Cardiff before a move to Aberavon. On his being capped, fellow villagers in his birthplace had clubbed together to buy Llew a watch and chain, presented at the Gwernymilwr Hall there. In 2010, Gill Jones headed the Aber Valley Heritage Group who magnificently clubbed together (again!) to bring the watch and chain home for display from a Chester auction.

Jenkins' departure for the Midlands had been part of the Welsh exodus to English light industrial centres in those decades: the other exodus was the familiar, well-trodden route to the North and the Rugby League, and

Llew Jenkins, Wales 1923: tribute and watch.

and

Llew's Welsh jersey and caps selection.

on January 7 the useful young wing Benjamin Davies gained a trial, only to join Hunslet RL the following day: the third back to go in four months. Still, two days later, Aberavon defeated Cardiff 12-8 with four tries before a crowd of 8,000.

Then, a week after playing against England, Brin Phillips moved to Huddersfield RL. Charlie Rowlands gained a cap in the win over Ireland but though selected against France, he was unfit and never again selected. To put things in perspective, though, Aberavon won a fierce match at Gloucester by 9-8 but home centre Sydney Brown was hurt tackling an Aberavon player. Though returning to play it was later found he had sustained a ruptured kidney and he died the following morning.

Aberavon had won at Bridgwater the previous day and two days after Gloucester they were at Torquay for a 10.30 am kick-off, returning to win at Penarth the following day, thus winning four away games in six days! When they lost to Pontypool on April 17, 1926 it was only their third home loss since December 27, 1919.

Welsh caps from Aberavon, 1923-24 to 1925-26: Aberavon RFC's capped players. Back row: Evan Williams, Lew Jenkins, Bryn Phillips, D. Hunt Davies. Front row: W.J. Hopkins, Bob Randell, T.D. Griffiths (Hon. Secretary), Willie James, C.F. Rowlands.

The first had come on December 27, 1921 to Cross Keys: then 43 unbeaten games until Maesteg on Boxing Day 1923 (what was it about Christmas?!) and 44 more unbeaten until that Pontypool reverse. Since the last days of 1921 Aberavon had played 88 home games with only one defeat, and the season finished: P 38, W 30, D 1, L 7.

Jack Jeremy became skipper for the 1926-27 season, which brought 17 wins in 20 outings to the end of 1926, including a return to Gloucester for a 13-6 victory. His pack included Rev H Jones and he had fine wings in Cyril Griffiths, son of the former secretary, and sprinter Harry Anderson.

Aberavon stormed on to a fourth successive Championship in this greatest-ever era. From January 1 they lost only 0-3 at home to Neath, and the season ended with a 27-5 win over Cardiff. April had seen another, even quicker, 'four away wins' show: this time in just five days, in an amazing spell of train travel and stamina.

Despite losing George Davies to Oldham RL in February, they finished P 44, W 36, D 4, L 4 (Points F 523 A 176), and into the Welsh pack for the final three games of the international season had gone the strong 22-yr-old E.M. ('Ned') Jenkins, who was to become one of the finest of all Aberavon players.

Another great character was explosive scrum half 'Tal' Harris, who was to win his cap (with Jenkins) against New South Wales at Cardiff in November 1927, but was never selected again. He was a docker and was said *'to have fought Russian sailors and ferocious dogs in Port Talbot Docks.'* Opponents on field must have been no trouble!

Evan John Stanley Davies – 'Stan' – was a huge character in the pack and he annoyed a Cardiff reporter so much in a 1927 trial that the critic said: *"Davies was constantly in front of the ball."* He was sent off for fighting with an opposing forward against Neath and when the pair went off they fought again with an intervening Vicar being knocked out in the brawl on the touchline!

One of Stan's tricks was to offer the ball to an opponent, then whip it away and race past him. He was Chris O'Callaghan's grandfather and was said to have blown fire from his mouth at spectators (while playing) and performed cartwheels along the touchlines. He was also a boxer who was reputed to have been fed sandwiches between rounds while fighting against opponents from travelling circuses and fairs.

He would win money 'to take his wife on a night out', though neither drank alcohol, or to boost the

Stan Davies.

Aberavon/Neath v NSW programme, 1927.

tour kitty. He went on the first-ever Crawshay's trek to Cornwall and became a life-long Wizards' servant: a club legend and committeeman for many years. However, though eleven times a reserve and a Final Trialist, he never won a full cap.

For 1927-28 and the gradual ebbing of the era it was: P 47, W 32, D 1, L 14 under captain and full back 'Dai' Williams, who on September 24 appeared against the touring 'Waratahs'. The NSW side, effectively Australia at the time, were met by an Aberavon/Neath team at the Talbot Athletic Ground.

It was the first time that Aberavon had hosted a touring team and a local brass band entertained though the rain poured down. The Mayors from both towns were present and 20,000 welcomed the tourists, who won 24-5 against a combined side with only six Aberavon players playing, as fly half Willie John Hopkins was unfit.

He had hoped to keep it a secret until just before the kick-off, so that club partner Harris could play, but the selectors were not in sympathy with the eleventh-hour drama and drafted in the Neath halves – together! The visitors led 6-0 at the interval, then wing Dan Jones (Neath) scored and Jack Jeremy converted, but the 'Waratahs' scored four tries with centre Cyril Towers outstanding.

'Ned' Jenkins was capped in all Wales' five-nation games, but there was tragedy for wing Cyril Griffiths, who had been called up by Wales along with Neath's Jones when Swansea's Rowe Harding withdrew. A last minute decision saw Jones play: Griffiths was never to gain a cap.

It might have been an ebb tide, but still in 1928-29 Aberavon finished runners-up in the Championship and 'Ned' Jenkins, Miah McGrath (the inspirational and characterful club captain), Stan Davies and Tommy Owen James played in a trial at Aberavon. It was to be seven years later that James was capped, while just as the second half began, Jenkins was sent off with the spectators bewildered: Wales selected him only against France.

On the same afternoon at Neath, a weakened Aberavon were thrashed 33-3, then, on an even sadder note, February 18 saw Sir Sidney Byass, so crucial and supportive a figure, die at his home in Llandough Castle, aged 66. The club he loved and so helped had a record for his final season of: P 40, W 25, D 6, L 9.

In May 1929 there was a reminder of some of what Bravon had lost northwards over the years, as Johnny Ring and Tom Parker were in the Wigan side who won the first-ever Rugby League Cup final to be held at Wembley. Tom had

Stan Davies and Miah McGrath pictured '50 years on'.

The great Johnny Ring in his Wigan Rugby League kit.

followed his brother Gwyn and so many others – from the area and further afield – in turning professional.

Despite that, there had been some real consistency from the club over a period of many years post World War One, with a magnificent peak, and many of its then-stalwarts were not only to be remembered with affection and admiration down the century, but also play a big part off the field after their boots had been hung or slung.

4

1929-49

Before the Balloon went up: and after.....

The Wall St Crash in America in October 1929 was to spark the Great Depression and see America catch a cold, Britain the flu and South Wales double pneumomia, but Aberavon's rugby fortunes, while not at the heights of the mid-twenties, survived the worst of the blows and saw some fine individual careers and successful seasons, while still suffering from regular departures to jobs (on or off the rugby field) over the border.

Miah McGrath, already building that reputation as one of the greatest clubmen, led again in 1929-30, with 'Ned' Jenkins playing in all four Wales games. The pair opposed each other in the November Welsh trial. It was not a memorable season, though, and after Neath had won at the Gnoll announced they were cancelling fixtures with Aberavon from the following season.

The side's 15-3 win at Guy's Hospital on February 8 was once more hailed by the English press as a splendid performance. The team was: Tommy James; Cyril Griffiths, Harold Hayes, E. Thomas, David Phillips; Wilf Selby, 'Tal' Harris; Miah McGrath (capt), Stan Davies, 'Ned' Jenkins, Walter Vickery, Will Owen, W. Davies, Gwyn Ridgeway, Arthur Bush.

David J. Phillips, wing on the day, went on to become a leading administrator, being Aberavon secretary, WRU member, international selector and Wales tour manager to South Africa in 1964.

Aberavon defeated Glamorgan Wanderers 22-3 in their first-ever meeting, while Hartlepool Old Boys were new visitors over Easter, as were Nuneaton two days later – both being beaten. The season ended with six games in 10 days to finish: P 40, W 20, D 3, L 17.

In 1930-31 'Ned' Jenkins was skipper and was to be so three times in the next four seasons. He was joined

Great Aberavon & Wales forward E.M. ('Ned') Jenkins.

Aberavon/Neath v South Africa - November 28th, 1931.
Back row: Mr. T.D. Griffiths, G. Prosser, A. Lemon, Supt. Rhys Davies.
Middle row (standing): Mr. P. Howells, G. Hopkins, M. McGrath, T. Arthur, W. Vickery,
E.M. Jenkins, Mr. W. Griffiths. Middle row (sitting): F. Nicholas, G. Moore, C. Griffiths
(capt.), P. Lloyd, G. Daniels, D. Jones. Front row: W. Selby, T. Harris.

by the powerful young Walter Vickery for a trial at Cardiff, but it was eight
years before Walter was capped.

It wasn't only the captain who struggled to gain favour and fashionability:
Cardiff played their second team against Aberavon on several occasions and
in September, *The Times* reported: *"Neath should be congratulated on settling
the dispute with THE CLUB FROM ABERAVON"(!)*

Secretary all the way, meanwhile, from 1921 to 1939 was Thomas Davie
Griffiths, a headmaster, who worked well with Willie Thomas (chairman)
and D.W. ('Printer') Jones (treasurer) to maintain that tradition of long-
serving, effective backroom workers. A poor onfield season, though, ended
for a change with four losses in the final 13 days: P 38, W 17, D 7, L 14.

Jenkins earned four more caps as champions Wales won three and drew
one of their international games, but Wales trialist Tom Gadd, a Glamorgan
Policeman, joined Cardiff during the summer of 1931. The captaincy passed

to Cyril Griffiths in 1931-32: he had 'retired' in April, only to come back as captain in September. A reporter stated: *"Cyril has found the secret of perpetual youth!"*

Griffiths, now playing as a wing forward, was skipper for the first 'Springbok' match to involve Aberavon, as the combined XV from Aberavon/ Neath famously held the touring South Africa to a close 3-8 scoreline at Neath, seven days before the Wales test in which 'Ned' Jenkins played. The 'Boks' had skipper Bennie Osler and Danie Craven at half back: as usual, it poured with rain as the referee from Pontyclun showed Craven how to put the ball into the scrum!

All the pits in the Dulais Valley had closed by 1.00pm so that many miners were amongst those who walked to the Gnoll. The Combined team, who wore white jerseys with a black Maltese Cros, led at the interval as Aberavon wing Fred Nicholas passed infield to Gordon Hopkins (Neath), who crossed.

Osler levelled with a penalty, though, drop-kicked from halfway, and three minutes from time, despite cries for a knock-on, Phil Mostert dived over. Osler converted amidst loud booing and the 'Boks acknowledged that this had been a hard-fought near thing.

Skipper Griffiths, who played in every position during his career, lived in Gower Street and as a youngster was an electrician at the Theatre in Talbot Road. He later wrote operettas, nativity plays and pantomines, all being performed at the old Wern Chapel, and formed a comedy partnership on stage with fellow player Brinley Davies.

Perhaps his on and off-field displays were appreciated by the members of the Aberavon Supporters Club which, after a 1920 attempt failed, had reformed, and they began producing the first official match programme. The club's return for a difficult season, though, was: P 41, W 17, D 4, L 20.

'Ned' Jenkins played for Wales in wins over England and Scotland, but after losing 10-12 to Ireland, heads rolled and he was not selected again. A new star, though, was wing Syd Williams, an under-15 cap against England at Cardiff. In a Dicky Owen benefit match at Swansea in April, Glamorgan Police were skippered by Jenkins and included centre Jack Thomas against a 'Welsh International XV' in which Walter Vickery played.

The faces were changing at the TAG and many of the great old guard had gone – if only to the stands – but the mighty 'Ned' Jenkins was to be skipper again in 1932-33. At fly half was usually David Owen, who was also a good sprinter and a fine bowls and tennis player who rejoiced in the title *'Mr. Rugby Football of Pontrhydyfen'*.

When Aberavon won at Guy's Hospital in December, however, they included a young fireball fly half in Tommy Egan, only for him to be eagerly snapped up by Oldham RL. At centre, 18-yr-old Randall Lewis paired with Jack Thomas and those three and scrum half Ifor Roberts, later a golf professional, all scored tries.

Allen McCarley from Port Talbot was 17 and a fitter and turner in the Steelworks, having come from Central School, but he moved to Neath to gain three caps in 1938 and was to have been their captain in 1939-40, only for war to intervene. He was back at Aberavon after the war and played against the 'Kiwis' in 1946 before becoming Aberavon's assistant coach and regular touch-judge.

Miah McGrath, that tremendous, big-hearted man who had also led Aberavon for two seasons, retired but remained in many other capacities, and also became a life member. His beloved club went 25 successive matches unbeaten until the final game against Llanelli on April 29. They certainly had admirers in the West Country, as *The Bridgwater Mercury* said:

"Aberavon has a beautifully balanced athletic machine, possessing strength and speed, ability and resource, alertness and agility in attack and all the doggedness of defence if it were needed. Aberavon have advanced throughout the season like the bore of a big spring tide. They have swept and swamped the pride of all from Leicester in the East to Llanelli in the extreme West."

Aberavon 1933-34, captained by E.M. ('Ned') Jenkins.

Not quite right about Llanelli, though – the loss meant that the Aberavon ground record lasted for 364 days and the season's tally was: P 48, W 30, D 6, L 12.

'Ned' Jenkins was again captain for 1933-34, but the campaign began badly, while in December Aberavon had another stamina marathon: a 'Christmas log-jam', maybe, as they played five games in nine days, including four in five. There was a recovery though, insofar as overall the record proved: P 43, W 25, D 1, L 17.

19-year-old Arthur Bassett from Kenfig Hill, and briefly Swansea, was switched to wing with great success. His brother Jack had skippered Wales and toured with the 1930 GB team to Australia and New Zealand. Arthur went on to gain a cap against Ireland in March, but the progress of such as him meant that Aberavon were often weakened by trial calls, despite the pack now including Griff Williams, the strong steelworker from Aberavon Quins.

In 1934-35, Aberavon finished runners-up in the unofficial 'championship', with full back Tommy Owen James as captain and new faces including wing Dennis Madden (soon to 'go North') and George Davies, who had played for Cheltenham and was to become secretary, and later chairman, after the war.

Bassett, meanwhile played three times for Wales, but his Police drafting to Barry was later to see him join Cardiff. On March 9, James, aged 30,

replaced the unavailable Vivian Jenkins for Wales in Belfast and placed a penalty in a 3-9 defeat. He was capped five years after his younger brother, Willie.

Half-back Wilf Selby was soon to join Rugby League while scrum half Stan Owen from Port Talbot County School was one of several to join Cheltenham. Alan Edwards was a wonderful wing from Kenfig Hill and looked certain to be capped but, aged only 18, he joined the Rugby League code, where he was capped by Wales and Great Britain.

In May a Wales XV met the Rest of Wales at Cardiff in a Royal Silver Jubilee match, with James (captain), Bassett and wing forward Ike Jones playing for the Wales XV while Walter Vickery, Randall Lewis, Edwards and Jack Thomas (a policeman who joined the Welsh Guards, was 2nd in the Welsh 100 yards and later became Aberavon captain) were in the Rest.

Wing Arthur Bassett in his British Police kit.

The final figures read: P 48, W 33, D 3, L 12, while 1935 also saw the Central Athletic Ground

Aberavon 1934-35, captained by T O James; Walter Vickery, middle of the 2nd row.

officially renamed as the Talbot Athletic Ground, the retirement of the great 'Ned' Jenkins and Jack Avery and Ike Jones (some said not for the first time!) being the latest to tread the 'Northern' road. Well, eastern, actually, for the League experiment in London.

In 1935-36 the new captain, Jack Thomas scored 37 tries – shades of Johnny Ring – and it was 'wringing' wet as the home game with Neath was abandoned after 65 minutes in extremely bad weather with Aberavon leading 6-3.

The clubs again combined to host New Zealand on December 14 at the TAG with eight Aberavon players, but could not match Swansea's shock win, losing 3-13. Tommy Owen James kicked a penalty in front of a 20,000 crowd, with some spectators on nearby mountain slopes lighting fires to keep warm.

Wing Alan Edwards at full speed for Salford RL.

Jack Thomas, Randall Lewis and Alan Edwards, 'Rest of Wales', 1935.

NEW ZEALAND

NEATH & ABERAVON
Talbot Athletic Ground, Port Talbot.

Complimentary
DINNER
TO OUR COLONIAL FRIENDS.

Lt.-Col. Sir GEOFFREY BYASS, Bart., J.P.
(President Aberavon R.F.C.) to preside.

GRAND HOTEL
PORT TALBOT
Saturday, Dec. 14th, 1935.

The menu card for Aberavon/Neath v New Zealand 1935.

Those All Blacks were the first team from New Zealand to come to Aberavon, and a week later they went down by a point to Wales, 13-12 at Cardiff. Another first – and last, for him, came in the home clash with Cross Keys. Evening Post reporter John Dolan, to whose earlier work we are indebted for a good deal of historical detail, was pulled out of the grandstand to assist the visitors when they arrived short!

Griff Williams, in some ways the new 'Ned' Jenkins, was capped against England, Scotland and Ireland, while a new forward was Ivor Heatley, another policeman who was to end up going east, to Cardiff for two years from 1936. At the time of his passing he was the oldest surviving Aberavon player. 1935-36, though, had added up to: P 42, W 24, D 4, L 14.

Walter Vickery emulated his father when he became captain for 1936-37 and a superb young fly half, Willie R. Davies, joined from Kenfig Hill, but moved to Cardiff in 1938-39, played in their Middlesex 7s victory and then turned to Rugby League. East then North! His brother was the much-loved Wales and 1950 Lions prop, Cliff Davies, also of Kenfig Hill and Cardiff.

A new face up front was the powerful Ray Hughes (whose brother Graham played for Neath). Centre 'Mog' Hopkins also appeared for Barnstaple and Devon, while Jack Thomas scored 18 tries and Tommy Owen James kicked 120 points. After playing in a Wales trial held at Aberavon, the classy centre Randall Lewis was the latest to switch to Rugby League, though.

The last 23 games brought 19 wins and four draws to total: P 45, W 30, D 8, L 7, and *The Times* called them *'The most improved side in Wales'*. James was capped against Scotland and in April Ivor Bennett was picked in the Wales pack in Belfast. It was postponed due to bad weather and he waited three weeks to play – and then some 40 years for his cap, as he also went north and had to wait decades for common sense and the amnesty to appear!

George Davies was captain for 1937-38 and when the club lost at home to Llanelli on September 27, it was after 29 unbeaten home games (W 25, D 4). The New Year brought 12 straight victories and despite a March loss at Pontypool after 18 wins and a draw, ten more wins followed to finish 'championship' runners-up with: P 45, W 37, D 2, L 6 (F 658 A 185).

Now a little older, flame-haired Syd Williams was outstanding at wing or fly half and scored 37 tries, with wing forward David M. James adding a further 14. Walter Vickery placed a goal from a mark at London Welsh, ran from his own half to score against Cardiff and was capped by Wales in all three games to follow – in a way – in the footsteps of his father, George, who was capped by England before Walter was born.

1938-39 found George Davies again skipper and Syd Williams touching down another 25 times. This was the last full season before the war, and though Aberavon finished runners-up in the Championship, the glory belonged to Syd, who marked being the first Aberavon player ever selected for the invitation outfit by grabbing four tries on his Barbarian debut, played in all three internationals and toured Cornwall with Crawshay's.

No future glories for him at the Wizards, though: by October 1939 he had gone to Rugby League with Salford. In January Arthur Bassett, now with Cardiff, joined Halifax and Ike Jones now DID go north, to Wigan.

Aberavon defeated Swansea on March 25, 1939, fielding: Tommy Owen James; Syd Williams, Jack Thomas, George Davies (capt), Roy N. Williams; L. Griffiths, D. Jennings; Walter Vickery, Edwin Kenifick, Joe Brothers, H. Willis, D. Griffiths, W. Davies, G. Thomas and

Ivor Bennett, Wales 1937 with his cap and jersey.

43

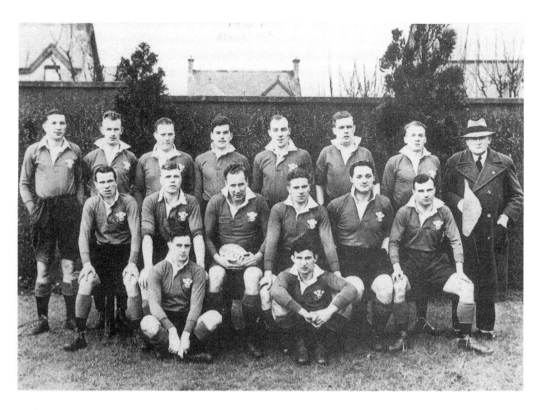

Wales in Ireland, 1939: Wing Syd Williams seated third right, next to skipper Wooller.

Ray Hughes, that side and their teammates assembling a campaign record reading: P 40, W 26, D4, L 10.

War loomed, but the 1939-40 season did begin, with hooker Haydn Williams as captain. However, games were restricted to those requiring little travel and Neath were met three times in five weeks. They played a fourth on December 30, when Aberavon won at home in what proved the only match played in Britain that day, due to very bad weather.

Aberavon/Neath were scheduled to combine to play Australia at Neath on October 28, 1939, but like all other games on the Wallabies' tour it was to be cancelled. Invasions other than that of the rugby men from Down Under were afoot; war was declared in the first week of the season and, having stayed at Penzance for most of their three weeks in the UK, the tourists went home without playing a single match, many to put on uniform and return to even harder action.

Only eight games were recorded from January 1 to April 20, 1940, including a 3-0 win at home to Neath. The 5-8 loss at home to Bridgend was the last official club match played until October 6, 1945, while Cardiff did not play Aberavon for a further 10 years.

No allotments on the Athletic Ground in this latest conflict: typifying the technological shift to air power in war, Aberavon's hallowed turf was used instead as a site for barrage balloons, intended to foil any anticipated Luftwaffe bombers' raids on the local docks and steelworks.

There were however some wartime games played by Services sides, and the following involved Aberavon players:

1940 – Ike Owens, Edwin Kenifick and Walter Vickery for West Wales v East Wales at Swansea.

1941 – Alan Edwards for the RAF v South Wales at Swansea. South Wales XVs often included wing Dennis Madden.

1942 – Syd Williams for S Wales v the Army; Madden for S Wales v Anti-Aircraft Command, both at Swansea.

1943 – Edwards (RAF) and Madden (South Wales) at Swansea; Williams for Army v Ireland at Belfast.

Stan Walter guested for Bridgend in the first visit to London in wartime by a Welsh club. Edwards and Owens for RAF v South Wales at Swansea; Randall Lewis for S Wales v the Army at Swansea; Arthur Bassett for a Midlands of England XV.

1944 – Williams for the Army v Ireland at Belfast and Scotland Services v RAF/Dominions at Myreside, with Owens and Edwards in the latter; Williams for the Army v S Wales at Cardiff; Bassett for Civil Defence v the RAF at Leicester and Bassett and Owens for S Wales v Dominions at Swansea.

Edwards and Owens for a RL XV that beat a RU XV at Bradford and the RAF v S Wales at Swansea; Bassett (then with Derby) played for South Wales. Owens for S Wales v the Army with Staff Sgt-Inst. Jack Thomas (Welsh Guards) for the Army. Thomas was a former club captain whose whereabouts thereafter are unknown. Did he die in the War or perhaps move to Workington RL?

Bassett for S Wales v NZ Services at Swansea and Williams for Scottish Combined Services v the RAF at Murrayfield.

1945 – Owens for RAF v the Army and British Empire Services v French Services at Richmond; Bassett for a Civil Defence XV, while Vickery played for Neath v the RAF with the proceeds to the War Comforts Fund of the Mayor of Neath.

1946 – Stan Walter for Dai Gent's XV v NZ Services at Chard.

> Among the Wales 1945-6 'Victory International' players were scrum half Billy Darch (Cardiff) and forward Sedley Davies (Maesteg), both later playing for Aberavon, while Sedley had also had a spell there pre-war. Both were granted WRU 'President' caps in 2013, but Sedley had died in June 1996 and Billy died shortly after the presentation.

With duty done, sacrifice suffered and another war over, rugby returned and Aberavon began on October 6, 1945 with a 'home' win (at GKB Sports Ground, Margam) against Abertillery. Vickery skippered, with secretary George Davies at full back, then on November 10, Maesteg became the first post-war visitors to the TAG for a 0-0 draw.

The Club's Players 'Capped' 1940-1946 (in Red-Cross/Services/Victory 'Internationals'):

Isaac Andrew (IKE) Owens – Born Pontycymmer 7/11/1918. Died Porthcawl 1988. Wing Forward. RL with Leeds/Castleford/Huddersfield / York/Wales/GB. Red-Cross 1940 (2); Services 1943 (1); 1944(1); 1945(1).

EDWIN Kenifick – Born Port Talbot 10/8/1914. Died 3rd quarter 1980, aged 66. Forward. Red-Cross 1940 (1).

ALAN Spencer Edwards – Born Kenfig Hill 15/5/1916. Died Canada 1986. Wing. RL with Salford (199 apps, 129 tries)/Dewsbury/Leeds/Bradford Northern (133 apps, 83 tries)/Wales (18 apps)/Great Britain (7 tries, 7 apps). Services 1942 (2); 1943 (2); 1945 (1).

SYDney Arthur Williams – Wing. Pre-war Wales cap. Services 1942 (3); 1943 (2); 1944 (2). (see Aberavon RU Caps section).

RANDALL D.Lewis – Centre. Died Port Talbot 6/9/2009, aged 95. RL with Swinton/Huddersfield/ Wales. Services 1943 (1).

Henry RAYmond Hughes – 2nd Row. Born 1920. Died @1998-99. Victory 1946 (1). His brother (Graham) played for Neath and also played in Victory internationals. In 2015 Ray's family received a WRU 'Presidents' cap, Ray having previously passed away.

When I asked Walter Vickery many years later how his bad hand and leg injuries allowed him to play, he replied: *"I was not really fit enough, as I had lost too many good years to the war. Though I had a few war-time games, it was six years before I was back in Aberavon colours. I knew I was not right, but had to give it one last go."*

Only nine games were played to the end of 1945 – W4, D 2, L 3. From January to May 1946 Aberavon fared little better – W7, D 1, L 9, but did meet one of the great 'touring' sides as on March 2, the 2nd NZ Expeditionary Forces played their last UK game of a long tour before a sell-out 19,000 crowd.

The 'Kiwis' won 17-4, though fly half Len Howard dropped a goal off the bar. Some things hadn't been changed by the events of 1939-45: he, too, soon joined Rugby League, and that 'Wizard' motif became fully established as part of the club's emblem.

Stan Walter had transferred to Cheltenham and Blackheath, while in the forwards, Allen McCarley had re-joined, but centre Joe Drew broke a collar-bone after 35 minutes. The great wing Jim Sherratt scored two tries and Bob Scott, who returned in 1953 with NZ, kicked a penalty and conversion.

The Kiwis' record in Britain, despite being as far from home as it was possible to be, and having come from the rigours of war (including three players from POW camps in Germany) was a hugely impressive P 27, W 23, D 2, L 2.

Two weeks later, Ernest Bevin, the Foreign Secretary, kicked off against Swansea. Both Neath matches were played on a Thursday and the final match, at home to Maesteg, saw the retirement of skipper Vickery.

A useful back and a talented player was Chris Wren, who also played for Bridgend, Kenfig Hill and an Idwal Rees XV against a University of Wales Past/Present XV in 1947. The University half backs were Denzil Jones (Cardiff University/Aberavon) and Haydn Tanner (Wales/1938 GB tourists).

For 1946-47 more of the old guard were back from service and some additional young talent showed promise. One pre-war player, David M. James became captain, former skipper George Davies was club secretary and Islwyn Morgan treasurer.

Trevor Lloyd had played at Eastern School in Taibach, then for SCOW and Cwmavon before Aberavon, but with Max Williams ultimately getting the nod at scrum half, it was from Maesteg, whom he was to skipper in their invincible season, that he won two caps in 1953 and made the Lions tour to South Africa in 1955. (He reached 91 in September, 2015, when he was the oldest-living Lion, but died a month later.)

There was little fire-power, though, and scores were low. Neath were beaten 13-12 in September, but the Welsh All Blacks won the next three by 10-0, 3-0 and 20-3; Llanelli won all four meetings and Swansea won home and away.

Danny Sheehy, Bob Jones and – ironically – Max Williams all turned to Rugby League, while the infamously bad weather of that snowbound

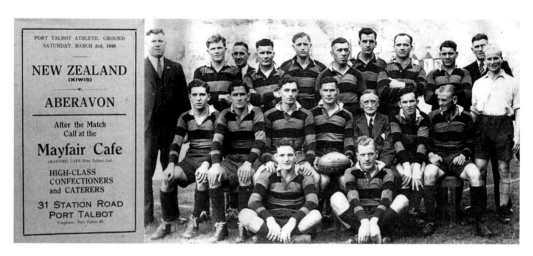

1946 Kiwis visit, and Aberavon 1946-47, captained by David M. James. Trevor Lloyd, later Wales & Lions, front left.

winter saw 10 games off and one abandoned and led to nine games being played in an 18-day period during April. (Nothing new for the Wizards!) So, the season's record was still: P 42, W 20, D 5, L 17.

Des Jones and Gwyn Martin had gained trial places, but then Jones moved to Llanelli and had a cap in 1948, skippering the Scarlets in 1949-50, while Martin went to Cardiff.

The highlight of 1947-48 under skipper and hooker Will Thomas was the Aberavon/Neath match against Australia at Neath in October. There were

seven Aberavon players selected, though Joe Drew withdrew. The Wallabies won 19-9 and the Combined XV played in Aberavon jerseys with prop Emlyn Davies scoring his side's only try.

Will Thomas may have scored if he had not collided with the referee, and the Combined side led twice before a brilliant try by centre Trevor Allan helped the Wallabies to 11-6 at the interval and they added two further tries after it.

Second row Bryn James was listed in the programme as Bryn

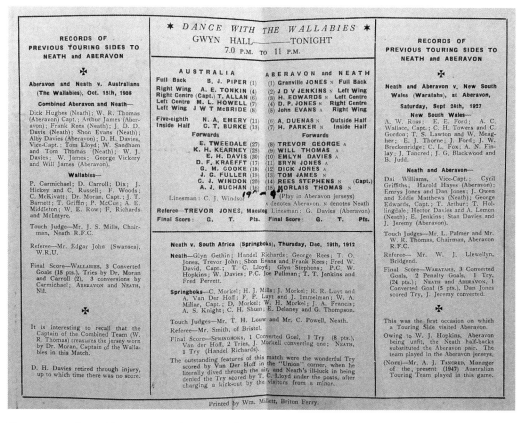

Team pages from Aberavon/Neath v Australia programme.

Jones. He came from Pencoed, joined the Welsh Guards in 1939 and was a PoW of the Germans for five years from May 1940. Returning home, work was short and he joined Whitehaven RL, playing against the 1952 Australian RL tourists and later returning to live in Porthcawl.

Wing Len Madden appeared for Notts, Lincs & Derby in the English Championship and ran so well for the Polytechnic Harriers that he finished second in the Welsh 100 yards Championships behind rugby international wing Ken Jones and was reserve for the 1948 Olympics.

September had seen Aberavon beat the Mayor of Port Talbot's XV on a Thursday and in December Emlyn Davies was called up to play for Wales against Australia and also appeared against Ireland in 1948. There were some good spells of rugby, including Neath being beaten 9-6 at the Gnoll, and fine newcomers including Brian Tashara, of whom more later, and wing John Evans, who switched to wing forward later in his career.

Emlyn Davies' cap 1947 vs Australia.

Emlyn Davies in a Crawshay's Welsh jersey.

David J. Phillips was secretary, W. R. Thomas chairman and J. I. Morgan treasurer of the club, whose season ended with a 21-14 win over an Enoch Rees XV and a final record which read: P 41, W 30, D 2, L9.

Joe Drew was captain for 1948-49, a campaign where many matches were nail-biters with just one score decisive, but the high point came on Boxing Day as Aberavon beat Neath by 17-5. Centre Gerwyn Rees (from Swansea) played in Welsh trials and equalled Johnny Ring's 1921 record of 21 points in a win at Briton Ferry in November.

Skipper Drew missed almost all the season after fracturing a cheek-bone in September and Emlyn Davies took control, while Rees received a shoulder injury early in 1949. Bryn James, Brian Radford (signed from Kenfig Hill) and Len Oates all switched to Rugby League, but the club still reached fourth in the Championship.

A young prop, Cliff David, was at Swansea University and played for Aberavon with RAF honours to come later. He began as a hooker, but when he opposed Will Thomas (the ex-Aberavon captain, then with Maesteg) he recalled: *"I won the first two balls, but Will was too wily and I was beaten so badly that I gave up thoughts of being a hooker."*

Cliff became club treasurer and a headmaster and still follows Aberavon every week along with the former chairman and medical officer, Dr Keith James, both being life members. Not everyone stayed: Aberavon captains Joe Drew, Will Thomas and David James all joined Maesteg making at least nine former 'Bravon' players already at Llynfi Road.

Just like the country, Aberavon fans were gradually getting somewhat better rations, with the club's return to good running rugby. This saw the emergence of the outstanding full back Ross Richards and a good centre in local Government surveyor Llew John while, in the pack, Albert Williams scored 12 tries.

Another addition was scrum half Billy Darch, now living in Port Talbot and being kept out at Cardiff by Haydn Tanner. His friend, Emlyn Davies, asked him to join the Wizards, which he did before his work took him to Alaska. His former home, Cardiff, offered two fixtures for 1950-51, symptomatic of Aberavon's standing, with a fourth-out-of-fourteen finish in the unofficial table for both 1947-8 and 1948-9.

John Evans scored 16 tries and fellow wing Tom Mainwaring 15, and April saw Aberavon defeat Swansea (5-0), Llanelli (11-5) and Neath (8-5

Aberavon 1948-49, captained by Joe Drew.

away) in a run of 12 wins and a 0-0 draw against Maesteg, to finish with a record of: P 41, W 29, D 6, L 6.

There was often a deal of fun off the field, with West Country tours, musical or not so tuneful renderings, duos, 'acts' and Tiller-Girls-style 'Aberavon Follies', plus games, competitions and concert parties with PE 'coach', organizer and impresario Bryn Thomas to the fore – as he was to remain.

Schools and/or Youth stars from the area in this era included scrum half David Onllwyn Brace, later Wales captain. He won Blues at Oxford and played for the RAF, Aberavon, Llanelli and Newport. Wing forward Rory O'Connor became club captain and a Wales cap, while Billy Pascoe played centre in the early 1950s and was the father of Swansea and Wales soccer forward Colin. Billy is from Taibach and his nephews, Adrian Bucknall and Andrew Bucknall, also played for Aberavon. Billy's mother came from the well-known Lodwig family.

The club was pleased to secure a renewed 50-year lease on 'their' ground, and during March junior clubs were allowed to play on it; and as the season ended, Emlyn Davies and John Evans, meanwhile, played for Captain Geoffrey Crawshay's Rest of Wales XV against Cardiff in the Gwyn Nicholls Memorial Match on April 28.

5

1949-1959

'The well-off problem child of Welsh club rugby'.....

Welsh prop Emlyn Davies led the side in 1949-50 and fellow prop Cliff David called him *"a gentleman":* Emlyn would often pick up an opposition player from the ground after a tackle or ruck. In later years he became Chairman of the club and was, until his passing in September 2016 aged 94, the oldest surviving Welsh international.

That season was a good one for Aberavon, including as it did four wins over Llanelli, the double over Neath, and if the Aberavon players and fans

1949-50

Back Row—Ken Davies, Cliff David, B. Tashara, A. Williams.
Second Row—I. Leyshon, D. T. Meredith, M. Williams, E. Vincent, E. Thomas, J. Sullivan, J. Mainwaring
Front Row— T. Mainwaring, W. Darch, Denzil Jones, E. Davies, R. Richards, Llew John, J. Evans.
(Vice-Capt) (Capt.)

ABERAVON R.F.C. 1950-51

Back Row—I. Leyshon, L. John, B. Phillips, L. Cunningham, R. Richards, D. B. Thomas.
Middle Row—D. J. Phillips (Hon. Sec.), E. Davies, C. David, D. T. Meredith, M. Williams, E. Vincent,
D. Jones, R. Jones, M. McGrath.

were to be believed, a home win over 'Invincible' Maesteg. However, the visitors' touch judge ruled otherwise and a 0-0 draw went in the books and into history for the Old Parish. Wing John Evans scored 14 tries and Tommy Mainwaring ten, while Ross Richards kicked 86 points. The final tallies were: P 43, W 28, D 8, L 7 and third in the 'table'.

John Evans became captain for 1950-51 and contributed a further 20 tries (and a drop goal), but the side lacked a good goal-kicker and the best news was that Cardiff were back on the fixture list, though Newport still chose not to be. Cardiff won 3-0 at Aberavon and then drew 3-3 at the Arms Park, being the first meeting for 11 years by Aberavon club records and 13 years by Cardiff records! Overall it ended: P 43, W 26, D 10, L 7.

Clubs were commenting that Aberavon's style had indeed changed to more running rugby, thanks in particular to 1951-52 captain Denzil Jones at fly half, who helped John Evans run in 27 more tries, while Ross Richards scored a then-club record 176 points. It was third place once more in the 'championship' with totals of P 47, W 36, D 4, L 7 including a 6-6 October

BRITISH XV v. ABERAVON
Monday, October 1st, 1951.

Today marks another milestone in the history of the Aberavon R.F.C. In opening the New Extension to the Grand Stand Aberavon can be justly proud of the progress they have made during the past 30 years. From the old ground at Sandfields where the spectators stood around the roped off playing area, we now possess one of the most compact grounds in the country. With seating accommodation for some 1,600 people and a covered Stand on the "tanner bank" we are now assured of a good gate whatever the weather. Today's ceremony will be performed by Mr. W. R. Thomas, O.B.E., Chairman of the Club, prior to the kick-off. Mr. Thomas has served the Aberavon Club, and rugger generally, faithfully for quite a number of years and it is fitting he should be asked to officially open the new wing.

These notes would not be complete without a word of praise for our hard working Secretary, Mr. D. J. Phillips, who during the past few weeks has put in a tremendous amount of work in getting together the British XV. He had many set-backs but, undaunted, carried on and succeeded in getting this galaxy of stars together. Thank you, Mr. Phillips.

To our visitors we extend a cordial welcome to Aberavon and trust they will look back on their visit as one of the highlights of their playing days. We are extremely grateful to all of them who in spite of the many calls on their services have come down to provide the opposition for this evening's game.

NEXT HOME MATCH—
SATURDAY, OCTOBER 6th—NEATH. Kick-off 3.30.

BRITISH XV v. ABERAVON

6 pts   Kick-off at 5.30 p.m.   6 pt

BRITISH XV		ABERAVON.
Full Back—		Full Back—
GERWYN WILLIAMS		1 Ross Richards 1 penalty
(Wales)		
Right Wing—		Left Wing—
D. H. PHILLIPS	**D. W. JONES**	2 John Evans
(Swansea and Final Trial)	**(Printers)**	
Right Centre—	**Ltd.**	Left Centre—
BLEDDYN WILLIAMS		3 Ll. John
(Wales and British Isles)		
Left Centre—		Right Centre—
LEWIS JONES 1 try		4 B. Phillips
(Llanelly and British Isles)	**Ring 229**	
Left Wing—	**for**	Right Wing—
MALCOLM THOMAS	**Efficient**	5 Ray Jones
(Wales and British Isles)	**Service**	
Outside Half—		Outside Half—
GLYN DAVIES		6 Denzil Jones
(Newport and Wales)		(Capt.)
Inside Half—		
HANDEL GREVILLE	**Courtland**	Inside Half—
(Llanelly and Wales)	**Place**	7 Arthur Evans
Forwards—	**Port Talbot**	
TOM PRICE 1 penalty		Forwards—
(Cheltenham and England)		8 Emlyn Davies
BOB ADAMS		9 Del Davies
(Cheltenham)		10 Den Jones
T. WRIGHT		11 Eric Vincent
(Cheltenham and Scotland)	Referee:	12 Cliff David
BEN EDWARDS	Mr. Trevor Jones,	13 A. Williams 1 try
(Newport and Wales)	Maesteg.	14 D. T. Meredith
DON HAYWARD		15 K. Davies
(Wales and British Isles)		
CLEM THOMAS		
(Swansea and Wales)		
ROY JOHN		
(Wales and British Isles)		
TED HORSFALL		
(Cardiff and England)		

Aberavon v International XV, 1951; captains are Bleddyn Williams and Denzil Jones.

1 draw against an International XV in a match to open an extension to the grandstand.

Teams: International XV:
Gerwyn Williams (W); Horace Phillips (W*), Bleddyn Williams (W/Lions) (rep: John Collins {Aberavon/W*}), Lewis Jones (W/Lions), Malcolm Thomas (W/Lions); Glyn Davies (W), Handel Greville (W); Tom Price (England), Bob Adams (Cheltenham), Terry Wright (Scotland), Ben Edwards (W), Don Hayward (W/Lions), Clem Thomas (W/Lions*), Ted Horsfall (England), Peter Evans (W).
   (W=Wales; *=capped later)

Aberavon:
Ross Richards; John Evans, Llew John, Bryn Phillips, Ray Jones; Denzil Jones (capt), Arthur Evans; Emlyn Davies, Del Davies, Denzil Jones, Eric Vincent, Cliff David, Albert Williams, David T. Meredith, Ken Davies.
   Referee – Trevor Jones (Maesteg).

v. Neath and Aberavon, November 17th. J. Du Rand, the tall Springbok forward gathers in a line-out and is about to pass the ball as tackled by two of the Combined XV.

Action from Aberavon/Neath v South Africa, 1951.

The game was marred by two WRU selectors ordering off 20 year old replacement John Collins after he had replaced the injured Bleddyn Williams in the sixth minute. Then John Evans retired with a shoulder injury and though it was a 'friendly' the WRU ruled 'no replacements'. Thousands of spectators booed the officials. Albert Williams scored a try and Ross Richards a penalty in the 6-6 draw.

There was a famous double over Cardiff, two out of three over Llanelli and in November Aberavon/Neath combined at the TAG to meet South Africa, whose great No 8 Hennie Muller led his side to a 22-0 win. The combined side's skipper, Rees Stephens (Neath), dropped out and Denzil Jones captained, but the 'Boks' were in top form and wing 'Buks' Marais scored three tries in front of a full house of over 20,000, with another 1,000 seated on Pen-y-Cae Hill – before the M4 was built!

The wrong music was played so there was no South African anthem. Their next game saw them thrash Scotland 44-0 – they must have been upset! Wing John Evans had already played against Australia in 1947 and was to appear at wing forward against New Zealand in 1954 to complete the southern hemisphere hat-trick.

One new fixture was against Rosslyn Park on London's Old Deer Park, with an 11.00am kick-off before England and Wales met at Twickenham. Aberavon won 15-8, with Roy Sutton at scrum half on loan from Swansea

Buks Marais scores one of his three tries.

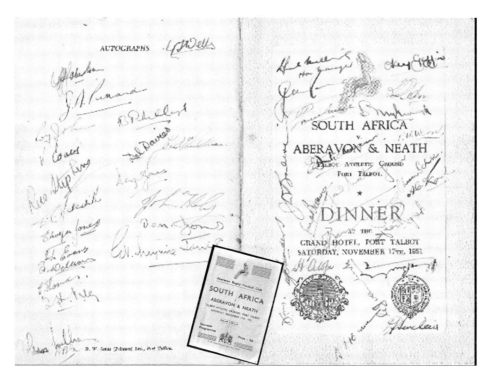

Menu and programme from the game.

as he was with Cliff David at Swansea University, while David Meredith was playing in the back row despite being listed as a Neath player in the match against South Africa.

After two draws with Neath, Aberavon won 19-5 at the Gnoll on St David's Day, then on April 14 the debutant Aberavon half-backs in a 14-6 win at Weston were Carwyn James and Onllwyn Brace! The season ended in style with 6-0 and 6-3 home wins over Llanelli and Cardiff.

These were the days of National Service, which for their two year call-ups kept many young rugby men very fit, gave them chances for services rugby, but deprived their home clubs of their regular availability. Flying Officer Haldon Lodwig, for example, played wing for the RAF against the Army, being stationed at St Athan during his service. He later became chairman of Aberavon.

Denzil Jones' second season as captain in 1952-53 was Aberavon's poorest since the war, but a fine result was the 11-9 home win over Cardiff, with John O'Sullivan scoring a try and Ross Richards a penalty, though it was 6-8 when lock Eric Vincent scored the winning try.

OFFICIAL SOUVENIR PROGRAMME

NEW ZEALAND
V
NEATH
and
ABERAVON
(COMBINED)
Chairman of Joint Match Committee
Mr. MELVILLE H. JOHNS

GNOLL GROUND, NEATH
SATURDAY, 23rd JANUARY, 1954

Kick off 2.30 p.m.

SIXPENCE

Aberavon/Neath v 1953-4 All Blacks programme.

There were also notable milestones. One was the return of fixtures with Newport; another, an invitation to be guests in the Middlesex Sevens at Twickenham. Aberavon beat the Woodpeckers 11-3 but lost 0-9 to London Welsh, who included Wales caps Bryn Meredith and Gareth Griffiths.

Also, the club later that year became the absolute owners of the TAG, and confirmed their shirt colours as red and black hoops. Shorts had also changed by now to white. At Twickers the Aberavon seven comprised: Keith Patten, Roy Bish, Douglas Griffiths, Onllwyn Brace; Ieuan Prosser, Del Davies and J. Thomas. Reserves: – Denzil Jones, Bryn Phillips, Ken Davies, David Owen and M. Joseph.

W. Keith Phillips played for Dorset & Wiltshire in the Championship and two props played for the RAF in the Inter-Services matches: Corporal Len Cunningham played against the Navy and Pilot Officer Cliff David replaced him against the Army. Prop Denzil Jones (another one!) joined Wigan RL (another one!) and Emlyn Davies skippered Crawshay's on their tour of Cornwall.

Merlin Williams was skipper in 1953-54 and Aberavon were said to be *'well off financially, but the problem child of Welsh club rugby'* in that it had such variations of form. In the ten years after the war the club had filled every position in the unofficial table between 3rd and 12th except 8th and 9th! It was also criticised for having far too big a selection committee, one of the old barbs thrown at the Welsh national set-up before the emergence of the Big Five (or, these days, Big One!)

It was not a great season, though Ross Richards scored 151 points, being top scorer of all the Welsh clubs. New faces included centre Roy Bish and wing Ken Thomas, while Glyn John (St Luke's College) won caps at centre and fly half and Cliff David played for the RAF against both Navy and Army and led RAF Yatesbury to the final of the RAF Cup.

Aberavon once more gained their best win of the season by 11-8 at Cardiff when tries came from John Evans and Keith Patten with Richards kicking five points. Former England forward, Dr. Cove-Smith, brought his team to gain an 11-6 win in September.

The combined Aberavon/Neath side put up fierce resistance to the All Black tourists at the Gnoll in January 1954. Nine Aberavon players were included with Glyn John at fly half, just a week after his international debut against England. The hosts scored 15 minutes from time when prop

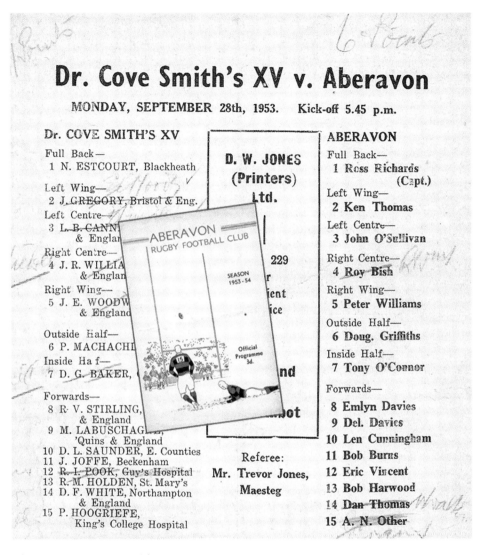

Dr. Cove Smith's XV v. Aberavon

MONDAY, SEPTEMBER 28th, 1953. Kick-off 5.45 p.m.

Dr. COVE SMITH'S XV

Full Back—
1 N. ESTCOURT, Blackheath

Left Wing—
2 J. GREGORY, Bristol & Eng.

Left Centre—
3 L. B. CANN
& Englan

Right Centre—
4 J. R. WILLIA
& Englan

Right Wing—
5 J. E. WOODW
& England

Outside Half—
6 P. MACHACHI

Inside Ha f—
7 D. G. BAKER,

Forwards—
8 R. V. STIRLING,
& England
9 M. LABUSCHAG
'Quins & England
10 D. L. SAUNDER, E. Counties
11 J. JOFFE, Beckenham
12 R. I. POOK, Guy's Hospital
13 R. M. HOLDEN, St. Mary's
14 D. F. WHITE, Northampton
& England
15 P. HOOGRIEFE,
King's College Hospital

D. W. JONES
(Printers)
Ltd.

229

ient
ice

Official
Programme
3d.

nd

ot

Referee:
Mr. Trevor Jones,
Maesteg

ABERAVON

Full Back—
1 Ross Richards
(Capt.)

Left Wing—
2 Ken Thomas

Left Centre—
3 John O'Sullivan

Right Centre—
4 Roy Bish

Right Wing—
5 Peter Williams

Outside Half—
6 Doug. Griffiths

Inside Half—
7 Tony O'Connor

Forwards—
8 Emlyn Davies
9 Del. Davies
10 Len Cunningham
11 Bob Burns
12 Eric Vincent
13 Bob Harwood
14 Dan Thomas
15 A. N. Other

Aberavon v Dr. Cove-Smith's XV programme, 1953.

Courtenay Meredith (Neath) stormed over and Ross Richards converted, only to lose 5-11.

Scrum half Onllwyn Brace moved to Newport, later representing the RAF, Oxford University and Llanelli and captaining Wales. The year's overall tally was: P 43, W 21, D 6, L 16, while in the first Welsh (Snelling) Sevens at Newport, Aberavon were 6-3 winners over guest side Bristol, but lost 3-6 to Llanelli in the quarter-finals.

Though centre Roy Bish led at the start of 1954-55, he lost both form and his place and moved to Neath, leaving scrum half Ken Jones – fittingly, the grandson of the club's first cap, Dan Jones – in charge.

The season started with a Bleddyn Williams XV winning 6-3 in a match to open the new clubhouse, as the Aberavon (Port Talbot) Athletic Club had taken shape (since extended) beneath the Grandstand. Now fans could drink, socialize and debate in their 'own' premises, one of the first of its kind in Wales. The Grand Hotel had previously been used by the club for entertaining their guests.

On November 20 Aberavon travelled to Gloucester for the first time in 20 years. The 'Wizards' won 16-3 with Cliff Ashton and Billy Pascoe scoring tries and Ross Richards kicking 10 points, while later, four games were won within five days, against Devonport Services, London Welsh, London Irish and the UAU. Almost the entire squad was under 30 years of age, and 27 of the 41 games were won, with a draw and 13 defeats.

Fears of any likely slump were dispelled by new captain Cliff Ashton and that young squad in 1955-56, but the start of 12 wins with only one reverse could not be sustained and Ashton himself lost form. September contained a match against a Bleddyn Williams XV to open the Willie R. Thomas and

Aberavon beat Auvergne in a tough game during 1955. The newspaper reporter wrote: 'There was a lot of tough forward play at the Talbot Athletic Ground between Aberavon and the French team Auvergne last evening. This line-out must have had the referee pondering about the obstruction law and whom to penalise.'

Humphrey Leyshon gates. That was won 6-3, as was the game with French visitors Auvergne, while Old Belvedere from Ireland were defeated 16-6 at home with away wins being gained at Cardiff (11-3), Swansea (11-9) and Neath (11-6).

Elfed Rees of the *Port Talbot Guardian* called the Auvergne game: *"The most murderous and barbaric game I have ever had the misfortune to witness."* It ended early, when French international second-row Bernard Chevallier clashed with 'Avon's Bob Burns, the latter being helped off by two team-mates and requiring stitches to his face.

In a concertina of clashes spectacular even by Aberavon's standards, four home games – Devonport Services, London Welsh, Neath and Llanelli – were played in successive days, producing three wins and a draw. Cliff Ashton and John Collins, who crossed, played for a Wales XV against a Lions XV at Cardiff and Keith Patten toured with the RAF to France and Portugal. The record finished: Overall it was 26 wins in P 44, W 26, D 6, L 12.

Cliff Ashton was captain again in 1956-57, and flanker Rory O'Connor, who had arrived from Bridgend, was capped against England at Cardiff. The club began with a 16-3 win over a Bleddyn Williams XV and a three-day trip to Ireland saw wins over Old Belvedere (13-9) and Bective Rangers (10-3).

December included a 9-6 win over Oxford University and despite losing to Neath on Boxing Day (3-6) and in March (3-5), both home, the side rebounded in April with a 30-11 success at the Gnoll. Ken Jones appeared for Surrey and the Harlequins and while Onllwyn Brace was captain of Oxford University, Tony O'Connor was set to follow him into the scrum half role there. Overall it finished: P 42, W 28, D 2, L 12, and the club reached the semi-final of the Welsh Sevens at Swansea before losing to Abertillery.

50s and 60s star Tony O'Connor.

Wales wing John Collins.

CLIFF ASHTON.

AN ALL-TIME GREAT ABERAVON RUGBY STAR.

Wales fly half Cliff Ashton.

John Collins was building a great reputation as both wing and pianist, including duets with skipper Ashton, while in that crucial behind the scenes work Jack Leyshon as masseur and Bryn Thomas as coach both continued to give great service, as did secretary D J. Phillips. Sadly, though, club chairman and former WRU president, Willie R. Thomas passed away and Alderman Llew Heycock took over in the former role.

Scrum half Tony O'Connor was aged 23 when he took the captaincy for 1957-58 – a season that saw debutant John Collins scoring the Wales try in a 9-3 win over Australia in January. He went on to play against England, Scotland and France in 1958, scoring tries in the last two. Secretary Phillips was now a Wales selector, too.

The combined Aberavon/Neath side lost 3-5 to Australia at the TAG on December 28, with Collins held back for Wales against the tourists a week later, though several of his clubmates played, including O'Connor as captain.

Versatile back and Glamorgan cricketer Alan Rees went to Maesteg and was capped four years later, but was then to switch to Rugby League. It was a good season with 10 games in September, including another match against a Bleddyn Williams XV, lost 5-6. October saw a trip to Ireland and a

Aberavon 1957-58, captained by Tony O'Connor.

9-6 win at Old Belvedere while the four meetings with Neath brought two wins, a draw and a loss. The record showed: P 42, W 24, D 9, L 9.

Len Cunningham led in 1958-59 and Aberavon reached November with W9,D2, plus a 0-3 loss at Llanelli. At home they defeated Old Belvedere 18-9 and a Bleddyn Williams XV 13-8 within three days and by December 31 the only home loss was 6-8 to Swansea, while the club beat Cardiff and Neath.

Collins played in all Wales' five nations games, Cliff Ashton joined him in the team and missed only the French match, while centre Haydn Davies, who was in the winning Cambridge XV against Tony O'Connor's Oxford, was capped against England and Scotland. O'Connor also helped his college, St Edmund's Hall, win the Oxford Colleges' Cup and London Welsh win the Middlesex Sevens. Hugh Thomas of Glan Afan Grammar School, a student at Cambridge, often played for the University, but just failed to gain a Blue.

Aberavon/Neath v Australia programme, 1957-58.

February saw the double over Cardiff, 8-0 away and on March 3 John Collins became the club's first post-war Barbarian and only the second-ever from Aberavon to play for the famous club, when he scored a try in a 21-8 win over the East Midlands. As the Fifties neared their end, his club's campaign tally was: P 41, W 28, D 3, L 10.

Aberavon RFC - Devon Tour 1958-59

6
1959-1969

Including another 'Wizard' time.....

As the 'Swinging Sixties' came round the corner, with the steelworks thriving, jobs about and the war becoming a more distant memory, for a number of seasons Aberavon might be have been forgiven for agreeing with Prime Minister Macmillan's contemporary assertion that 'You've never had it so good'. Rather like that decade's plans to make Aberavon Beach a resort to rival Barry and Porthcawl, however, it started better than it finished.

Captained by Len Cunningham, the club finished fourth in the 1959-60 Championship, having opened with seven wins in nine matches. There was a short tour to Fylde and New Brighton in March, and the best win came in April by 19-8 at Neath. September 5 had brought the debut of back-rower Roger Michaelson, while Roy Bish returned from Neath but later moved to coach at Cardiff. Overall it was: P 45, W 28, D 6, L 11.

The Aberavon team, captained by Rory O'Connor, that won the Welsh Championship in 1960-61.

John Collins, Cunningham and Cliff Ashton played for Wales against England, the latter pair against Scotland and Ireland, with Cunningham also appearing against France. In the Welsh Sevens, Aberavon lost 10-11 to eventual winners Llanelli in the semi-finals.

Chris O'Callaghan, himself the diametric opposite of a shrinking violet, commented: *"Rory O'Connor and Peter Jones were my first memories in the early 1960s. They terrorised opposition half backs like Cliff Morgan. I loved them."* Cliff agreed: though not about loving them!

Rory O'Connor took over as captain for 1960-61 and was a great success in a campaign where the club won the unofficial 'Welsh Championship' for the first time since 1927, with final figures of P 48, W 40, D 4, L 4. Points: F 738 A 191, scoring 155 tries with only 30 against.

The achievement was due in part to remarkable fitness and team spirit, with several games won in the closing minutes as they outlasted their opponents. Big-boot full back Kel Coslett from Bynea set a club record of 188 points and wing Ken Thomas scored 26 tries, while centres David Thomas and Brian Jones each scored 20.

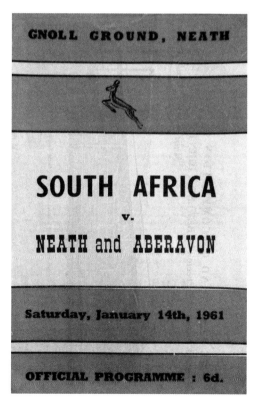

The biggest defeat was at Exeter by 8-16 on March 14, and a home defeat by Cambridge University marked the opening of Aberavon's new floodlights. There was a 12-6 win at Cardiff; fine doubles including Swansea, Gloucester, Bridgend and Pontypool; two wins and two draws against Llanelli and three wins in four clashes with 'old enemies' Neath. The season ended with eleven successive victories.

On January 14 at Neath, though, an Aberavon/Neath side, containing six backs and two forwards from Aberavon, but with internationals Coslett and Cunningham held back, were well beaten 25-5 by the powerful South African tourists. The Gnoll was full to capacity but the 'Boks' scored six tries against a solo by Tony O'Connor and remained unbeaten until their final match in Britain when the Barbarians won 6-0 at Cardiff.

Aberavon/Neath v 1960-61 S Africa programme.

Wales centre David Thomas and prop Phil Morgan, 1961.

Roger Michaelson played for Cambridge, both in the Varsity match and against South Africa. Tony O'Connor had played for Wales against the 'Boks in the 'Day before the Deluge' Arms Park defeat, and he and Phil Morgan, then Wales' youngest prop cap, also appeared against England and Scotland, David Thomas against Ireland and John Collins and Morgan against France. Through the Heycock good offices, the whole squad celebrated at County Hall, too.

Rory O'Connor was again captain for 1961-62 (though he suffered injury) and in mid-November there had been just one reverse, to Cardiff, in 18 outings. Overall it finished: P 49, W 33, D 4, L 12 with a

Champions Aberavon at Glamorgan County Hall, May 1961.

Aberavon 1961-62, (Kel Coslett 4th right at back, Tony O'Connor, Rory O'Connor (capt.), Cliff Ashton and John Collins front, 2nd left to 2nd right) & programme.

creditable fourth place in the 'Championship', and a satisfying 24-0 home win over Neath.

At Clifton College, Bristol, an Old Boy, Roger Michaelson, led Aberavon to a 23-8 win over a West of England XV to celebrate 100 years of rugby at the College. Aberavon played what had increasingly become their trademark, a superb running game with *The Times* newspaper describing them as *'the best side in Wales'.*

The teams were: West of England (W=Wales; E=England) – A. Lewis (Clifton); Jim Glover (E), Harry Morgan (W), Ricky Bartlett (E), Gordon Wells (W); Graham Powell (W), Dickie Jeeps (E); L. Jenkins (Bristol), Roger Whyte (Harlequins), Ron Jacobs (E), Vic Leadbetter (E), R. J. Bradford (Clifton), Nick Silk (later E), David Coley (Northampton), D. C. Mills (Harlequins).

Aberavon – Kel Coslett; John Collins, Brian Jones, David Thomas, Ken Thomas; Cliff Ashton, H. J. Williams; Len Cunningham, Rhys Loveluck, Phil Morgan, B. Thomas, John Bamsey, Alan Bamsey, Roger Michaelson (capt), Peter Jones.

Referee: N. Wyatt (Bristol).

Michaelson played in the Varsity match, while Tony O'Connor played for Wales against France and in ten matches for the British Lions in South Africa during the summer of 1962 – Aberavon's first-ever Lion.

Coslett and Cunningham appeared for Wales against England, Scotland and France with the Ireland game being put off until November due to a smallpox outbreak. Tony O'Connor played for the Barbarians against

67

Tony O'Connor kicks for the 1962 Lions in S Africa.

East Midlands, the durable Billy Hullin was a new scrum half alternative, but Coslett moved to Llanelli for 17 games in 1962 before signing for St Helen's RL on July 6. Even in the 'good times', the lure of the League stayed strong and the cheques grew larger.

Wales skipper Clem Thomas said: *"Aberavon are a side with no apparent weaknesses, proud of their achievements and playing with an ebullience which most sides will find hard to contain."* Of wing forward Peter Jones, Thomas added: *"He is a tearaway whom most players would rather play with, than against."*

In these very early days of coaching, Bryn Thomas was still proving invaluable, Born in Port Talbot and educated at Wycliffe College, he was a PTI sergeant in the RAF, gained a silver medal at hockey in the 1948 Olympics and the BEM and became a life member of the club in 1972.

In later years he commented: *"There will always be a tomorrow with Aberavon, who, through the years, have been ever steadfast and progressive. I salute them and wish them all the very best for those tomorrows".* Chris O'Callaghan said: *"He was a pretty remarkable man, an achiever, a man with huge self-confidence, a relentless self-promoter, but nevertheless a tireless worker for Aberavon. No history would be complete without reference to him."*

Len Cunningham became captain for the third time in 1962-63, a season which saw December and January virtually frozen off. There was a 21-0 win at the Gnoll and 10-3 over Cardiff with superb tries by Hullin and David Thomas, while the away match in February was drawn 6-6 with Dennis Perry and Michaelson crossing for tries.

The game at London Welsh on December 15 was the first meeting at Old Deer Park and the first between the clubs in London since 1938-39 at Herne Hill. Former 'Wizard', Haydn Davies, was the Exiles' fly half while

Cardiff are the visitors to the Talbot Athletic Ground.

full back Graham Young, from Llanelli, scored Aberavon's try in the 3-6 loss.

There was a 10-10 home draw with Cambridge University before the double was completed over London Welsh but the campaign ended with a 39-point mauling by Llanelli at Stradey Park, making the overall picture: P 46, W 31, D 5, L 10. This was the first season for young doctor Keith James, who became a life member and was still supporting Aberavon 54 years later.

Tony O'Connor played for the Barbarians at Leicester, while the delayed '1961-2' Wales match in Dublin included Cliff Ashton, O'Connor and Cunningham. Michaelson won his only cap against England and skippered Cambridge in the 1962 Varsity match.

In May, Aberavon travelled to Germany and at the Olympic Stadium in Berlin defeated the Combined Services 28-8, then four days later beat a 'Wales in Germany' XV 60-3. The party was billeted at the Spandau Barracks, near the notorious fortress prison. The actual playing field used at the Olympic Stadium was where the equestrian section of the 1936 Olympics had taken place.

Roger Michaelson, Wales 1963.

Aberavon/Neath v 1963-64 All Blacks - jersey & programme.

Prop Phil Morgan took over the captaincy for 1963-64, but Rory O'Connor retired after a knee injury and Cliff Ashton took a job in Llanwern, site of the 'newer' steelworks (now closed!), living in Chepstow and playing for Cardiff. Billy Hullin also joined Cardiff and fine hooker Rhys Loveluck left, while John Collins retired after scoring 122 tries, just three short of Johnny Ring's club record. Still there, though, was the tireless policeman Omri Jones, terrifying opposing fly halves.

Wilson Whineray's All Blacks were touring and Aberavon/Neath played a trial against London Counties under the Aberavon floodlights on October 23, winning 10-3. Nine days later, they included 14 of that team to meet the All Blacks, including eight 'Wizards' with Morgan as captain.

A crowd of 10,000 had watched the London game and an estimated 21,000 crammed into the TAG to see New Zealand win 11-6. The rain and mud was so great that it was impossible to see whether Len Cunningham or Peter Jones had gained a touchdown. A Grahame Hodgson (Neath) penalty made it 6-3, but the tourists, who included Don Clarke and his brother Ian, the Meads brothers and Waka Nathan, scored three tries. So bad were conditions that no club game would have taken place and the five Aberavon backs took little part in it.

Cunningham played for Wales against NZ as well as in all four Championship games and for the Barbarians against NZ at Cardiff. He also made the Wales tour to South Africa in 1964 and played in the test. Haydn Davies (by then at London Welsh) was also in the tour party, managed by David J. Phillips who sadly and suddenly died soon after.

Roger Michaelson appeared twice for London Welsh against Aberavon, opposing Billy Mainwaring (at No. 8) in the game at Old Deer Park. The statistical summary was P 44, W 23, D 3, L 18 with an 8-3 loss to an International XV.

Aberavon were captained in 1964-65 by their splendid centre Brian Jones, but it was not a good season because although English clubs were generally beaten, Welsh opposition was not. Neath won three of the four meetings with one draw; Cardiff ran in six tries in a 24-3 win and joined Newport and Bridgend in beating the 'Wizards' twice.

Billy Mainwaring was sent off at London Irish, though Aberavon won 18-9. He was automatically suspended, but later the WRU found him not guilty! There was a 9-6 win over Cambridge University in March and London Welsh were beaten 29-11 in April.

Chris O'Callaghan said: *"As I grew up, Billy WAS Aberavon Rugby Club. He was a fantastic example of a tough, hard, wholly uncompromising forward who through his actions on the field and the way he lived his life demanded respect from friend and foe alike. I didn't play many games alongside him (I wasn't fit to tie his bootlaces) but the few that I did, were an honour, a privilege and an enormous pleasure. He is a legend and I am humbled by the fact that I was able to share the same dressing room and the same field as him."*

The experimental, try-driven midweek Floodlit Alliance had begun and Aberavon won it in this, its second year, by beating Bridgend in the final on a 34-17 aggregate – winning 28-8 at home and losing 6-9 away. Among the new faces in the club squad was Bobby Wanbon, who began as a prop before moving to No.8.

Across the season it went: P 44, W 19, D 5, L 20, and at representative level, when a Wales XV broke new ground by meeting those ever-entertaining runners, the touring Fijians at Cardiff in 1964, David Thomas at centre scored a brace of tries.

The powerful lock Max Wiltshire was the skipper for 1965-66, a season which saw Aberavon lose 20 games yet never concede more than 18 points. The 69-6 victory over Aberavon and District was the club's highest-ever score, but there was an amazing loss at Chepstow, while the match at home to Swansea in November was abandoned after 35 minutes, due to heavy snow.

Australian-born Wales lock Max Wiltshire.

There was an 11-6 win over Cambridge University and hopes were high for all-action flanker Omri Jones after he ousted British Lion Haydn Morgan from the Probables side in the Final Trial, but Morgan still played in the internationals. Omri had been sent off early in the season while playing as a centre. The first-ever WRU National Sevens were played at the TAG, with Pontypool Utd. proving the winners. Aberavon's campaign concluded: P 47, W24, D 4, L 19.

In 1966-67 Max Wiltshire was again captain and new faces included centres Ian Hall and Francis Reynolds, the former Wales Youth, Tumble and Llanelli hooker Morton Howells and the Police wing Ron Staddon. There was also, pleasingly, a promising crop of youngsters including Wales Secondary Schools full back Paul Wheeler and Under-15 and Youth cap, winger Robert Fleay.

In addition, the club could call on Mike Nicholas: dynamic, blond-haired, play-anywhere with a smile that hurt if you were on the opposing end of his tackles. 'Mikey Nick' started as a scrum half, went back to Aberavon Green Stars, but returned as an open-side wing forward.

Australia, with ace scrum half Ken Catchpole taking the captaincy, met the Aberavon/Neath side at The Gnoll. Jim Lenehan kicked all the points in a 9-3 win against a try by Dai Morris (Neath). Seven Aberavon players were in the combined side, with Billy Mainwaring at No 8.

Aberavon achieved the double over Cardiff, and in the away win it was two late drop goals by fly half Bernard Locke which won it. On October 12, Aberavon lost 5-6 to an International XV at the TAG in a match to open the David Phillips Lounge. Two Aberavon players, one defying identification, were drafted in to replace fly half Peter Rowe (Swansea) and prop *Ron Waldron (Neath).

The 'International XV' was (*=Wales): Glen Landeg (Bridgend); *David Weaver (Swansea), *Keith Bradshaw (Bridgend), John Davies (Swansea), *Peter Rees (Newport); Lyn Willis (Aberavon), *Clive Rowlands (Swansea); *Denzil Williams (Ebbw Vale), Roy Thomas (Swansea), 'unknown' (Aberavon), *Brian Thomas, Jeff Pyles (both Neath), *Gary Prothero (capt), Colin Standing (both Bridgend), *Dai Hayward (Cardiff). Referee: Meirion Joseph.

Aberavon/Neath v All Blacks programme, 1963.

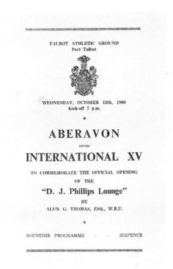

ABERAVON
1966 - 67

The Wales Secondary Schools lock Allan Martin made his debut in September, then won his spurs as a senior player (when Mainwaring was injured) against Neath in December. He retaliated to Brian Thomas at the urging of Max Wiltshire, and recalls: *"Until then I was just a tall lineout jumper, but when I punched Brian at the first lineout of the second half, I never had problems with him again!"*

'Billy' (Gwilym Thomas on his birth certificate, W T in programmes) Mainwaring played in all the five nations games, Roger Michaelson became a Barbarian at Leicester and a young Phil Bennett played in six matches on loan from Llanelli. The WRU National Sevens final at Aberavon saw Cardiff College of Education victorious. The overall record was to read: P 47, W 29, D 5, L 13 for a fifth spot in the unofficial 'table'.

Cyril Jones was captain for the 1967-68 season and enjoyed a good start with only one defeat in the first 14 matches, but in the New Year losses mounted and overall there were only 18 wins: P 39, W 18, D 5, L 16.

Billy Mainwaring played for the Barbarians against Leicester (as No. 8) and East Midlands (as lock), while Max Wiltshire was a Barbarian against Cardiff, Newport and NZ (at Twickenham). The pair

Legendary locks Billy Mainwaring and Allan Martin.

An 'Avon' trio in Wales' 1968 training & playing pack at Twickers.

both appeared for Wales against NZ in 1967, as did new caps Ian Hall (in his first full season) and full back Paul Wheeler.

Mainwaring, Wiltshire, Wheeler and debutant Bobby Wanbon all played against England, with Wanbon scoring a try but being dropped. Wiltshire also played against Scotland and France, while Wanbon and Cyril Jones played for West Wales against the All Blacks at Swansea.

The WRU National Sevens was again held at Aberavon and won by Llanelli.

Wanbon, watched by teammate Billy Mainwaring, scores for Wales in his first international.

Wanbon, the Supporters' Club's first recorded Player of the Year, annoyed at being dropped by Wales, joined Warrington RL in February, but prop Jim Anderson (a Wales under-23 cap from Maesteg) then joined the pack.

In the summer of 1968 locks Wiltshire and Mainwaring toured with Wales in the Argentine, playing together against a Provincial XV and in the 2nd 'Test', while Wiltshire also played against a Combined XV and Mainwaring against Belgrano and in the 1st 'Test'. No caps were awarded then, though both had of course already received that honour. Uncapped players whose only 'Test' was against Argentina received 'President's caps' decades later.

For 1968-69 the club turned to loyal hooker Morton Howells as the new captain. Howells was from Tumble,

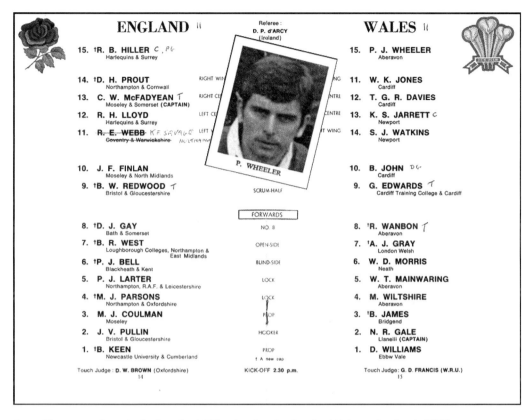

ENGLAND		Referee: D. P. d'ARCY (Ireland)		WALES
15. †R. B. HILLER C P6 Harlequins & Surrey			15.	P. J. WHEELER Aberavon
14. †D. H. PROUT Northampton & Cornwall	RIGHT WIN	NG	11.	W. K. JONES Cardiff
13. C. W. McFADYEAN T Moseley & Somerset (CAPTAIN)	RIGHT CE	NTRE	12.	T. G. R. DAVIES Cardiff
12. R. H. LLOYD Harlequins & Surrey	LEFT CE	ENTRE	13.	K. S. JARRETT C Newport
11. R. E. WEBB KF SAVAGE Coventry & Warwickshire Nυττιη nν	LEFT V	T WING	14.	S. J. WATKINS Newport
10. J. F. FINLAN Moseley & North Midlands			10.	B. JOHN DG Cardiff
9. †B. W. REDWOOD T Bristol & Gloucestershire	SCRUM-HALF		9.	G. EDWARDS T Cardiff Training College & Cardiff
		FORWARDS		
8. †D. J. GAY Bath & Somerset	NO. 8		8.	¹R. WANBON T Aberavon
7. †B. R. WEST Loughborough Colleges, Northampton & East Midlands	OPEN-SIDE		7.	¹A. J. GRAY London Welsh
6. †P. J. BELL Blackheath & Kent	BLIND-SIDE		6.	W. D. MORRIS Neath
5. P. J. LARTER Northampton, R.A.F. & Leicestershire	LOCK		5.	W. T. MAINWARING Aberavon
4. †M. J. PARSONS Northampton & Oxfordshire	LOCK		4.	M. WILTSHIRE Aberavon
3. M. J. COULMAN Moseley	PROP		3.	¹B. JAMES Bridgend
2. J. V. PULLIN Bristol & Gloucestershire	HOOKER		2.	N. R. GALE Llanelli (CAPTAIN)
1. †B. KEEN Newcastle University & Cumberland	PROP † A new cap		1.	D. WILLIAMS Ebbw Vale
Touch Judge : D. W. BROWN (Oxfordshire) 14	KICK-OFF 2.30 p.m.			Touch Judge : G. D. FRANCIS (W.R.U.) 15

Four Aberavon stars, including Paul Wheeler, inset, play for Wales v England, 1968.

where he had gained 1958 Youth caps against France and Germany, and moved from Llanelli when Norman Gale joined that club.

He was a fine leader, a marvellous clubman and became a life member who was still to be seen working on the gate of the club nearly 50 years later, having led Aberavon to two cup finals as well as playing for the Barbarians.

After a good September, the team fell away despite wins over Cardiff (6-3 home) and Neath (11-9 away). Then came the real cruncher, as London Welsh were visitors on Easter Saturday and handed out a biggest-ever 8-52 beating: yet the 'Wizards' had defeated Northampton 19-6 the previous day, drew at Neath two days after the 'Exiles' defeat and soon beat Bristol 22-3.

Aberavon finished 13th in the 'Championship' with a record of: P 41, W 19, D 2, L 20, and wing Robert Fleay scored 21 tries. Llanelli won the Floodlit Alliance, even though they had lost 3-12 to Aberavon at Stradey Park.

7

1969-1979

Cometh the Cup. Finals, two: luck, nil!.....

Man may have first stepped onto the moon in the close season of 1969, but there was no giant leap forward for the Wizards for the next few campaigns. Despite some good wins, there were also a lot of stiff losses in the 1969-70 campaign under skipper Billy Mainwaring. The worst was by 8-39 at Northampton, the Saints later completing the double.

Argentinian club San Isidro came in October and Aberavon won a bruising match by 17-3, but though the Aberavon/Neath side were expected to run the apartheid-protest beleaguered South Africans close at Aberavon, the 'Boks', led in this match by Tommy Bedford, won 27-0. Billy Mainwaring skippered the combined side from second row and seven of his club colleagues also played.

Aberavon centre John Simonson was playing at No 8 before the season ended, but the move for centre Francis Reynolds and wing Bob Fleay was a step further: both were to switch to Rugby League, Fleay going in October 1970.

Ian Hall had said he did not want to be considered as a wing – so both the combined side and Wales selected him there! He played for a Wales XV to open London Welsh's clubhouse in October; for East Wales (with a try) against West Wales at Cardiff and was capped by Wales against South Africa, Scotland and England.

TALBOT ATHLETIC GROUND, PORT TALBOT

ABERAVON - NEATH

versus

SOUTH AFRICA

WEDNESDAY, 10th DECEMBER 1969
Kick-off 2.30 p.m.

Aberavon/Neath v South Africa programme, 1969.

One notable win was by 14-0 home to Cardiff in January, March brought an 8-6 verdict at Newport and a 14-3 success against Neath; Swansea were beaten in April by 30-9. Aberavon finished with a record of: P 45, W 23, D 3, L 19, after six wins in the final seven matches.

Aberavon Supporters Club, a valuable aid over so many years, then had Moel Evans as chairman Fred Lucas as treasurer and Bill Lewis as secretary, and they had to grit their teeth somewhat as 1970-71, with Mainwaring again captain, was poorer. The opening match was lost at home to Taibach by 3-12 amid a staggering 17 games played in September and October with another 17 in March and April: the 'good old days', eh?

There was a win over Frenchmen La Rochelle by 19-5, nail-biters over Swansea (9-6), Neath (6-5) and Llanelli (9-6), but losses by 0-33 at Llanelli, 11-36 at Cardiff, 5-41 home to London Welsh and in the three other games with Neath, while the last six games were all played away. P 46, W 21, D 3, L 22 made it a less than 50% record overall.

Ian Hall and Allan Martin appeared for a WRU President's XV against Cardiff and for Wales Under-25's (remember them?) against Fiji, with Hall scoring a try in the latter and also playing for Wales in the memorable Murrayfield match as part of the 1971 Grand Slam.

In the National Sevens at Cardiff, Aberavon reached the final only to lose 8-23 to Llanelli. Condon scored two tries in the final (including, since this was in August, the last three-point try in Wales), and the dynamic Mike Nicholas placed the final conversion to add to his eight previous goals and a try

Hall was made captain for 1971-72, a season which saw both the four-point try and the WRU Knockout Cup introduced. In the latter, Aberavon made the semi-finals by defeating Nantymoel 44-0, Penclawdd 16-6, Bridgend 15-3, Newport 28-6 (all home) but lost 7-13 to Llanelli in a semi-final at Swansea – mostly because hooker Morton Howells dislocated an elbow after 34 minutes.

The dislocated shoulder of splendid fly half John Bevan saw 30-year-old former Bridgend and Wales centre Ron Evans being borrowed from South Wales Police to help in the quarter and semi-finals.

GNOLL GROUND, NEATH

NEW ZEALAND

v.

NEATH & ABERAVON
(combined)
KICK-OFF 2.30 P.M.

Wednesday, 24th January, 1973

OFFICIAL SOUVENIR PROGRAMME
10p.

The Aberavon/Neath v All Blacks programme, 1973.

Ian Hall.

Hall played against Neath for both the WRU President's XV and the Barbarians and Allan Martin played for the latter against Penarth and Cardiff. Clive Shell was in the WRU President's team and both Martin and Dennis Curling played for Glamorgan under-25s against Canada.

Martin scored 147 points and schoolteacher David Condon from Aberavon Green Stars ran in 22 tries (playing wing and flanker), while Curling equalled the club record of seven tries in the Cup win over Nantymoel. Overall, it finished: P 41, W 20, D 2, L 19.

Aberavon centre and schoolmaster Malcolm Swain scored a try for Moseley against winners Gloucester in the first English cup Final. He also appeared for St Luke's College and was soon to become the first man to play in both the English and the Welsh cup finals.

In 1972-73 hooker Morton Howells, a GPO mechanic, clearly hadn't got his wires crossed as his side enjoyed a good season under his captaincy, though the Cup exit came quickly with a 6-10 home defeat by Newbridge.

The New Zealanders were on tour, and as usual, Aberavon/Neath failed to play well together as a team and were pasted by 3-43 at Neath on January 24. Then-emerging rugby balladeer and Dai Morris-worshipper Max Boyce summed up the relationship:

> '.....Neath blamed Aberavon, and Aberavon, Neath;
> Some they blamed the weather, and some blamed you and I,
> And some they blamed the referee: but no-one there blamed Dai!'

Full back Joe Karam scored 19 points and the tourists ran in seven tries against a lone Allan Martin penalty. John Bevan had withdrawn with a knee injury and three days later came the famous Barbarian win over NZ by 23-11 at Cardiff. Ian Hall had transferred to South Wales Police and he opposed the tourists for East Glamorgan at the Arms Park.

Despite losing Mike Nicholas, Clive Jones and Dennis Curling to Rugby League and Billy Mainwaring to a broken collar-bone, Max Wiltshire returned from Bridgend, Clive Shell was outstanding, full back Mike Francis from Felinfoel kicked 125 points and Martin 136, with tries coming from wing Huw Jenkins (16) and centre David Prendiville (14).

There was a double over London Welsh, a 35-9 win at Neath and Bristol were pounded 39-13 with Shell scoring three first-half tries as the Wizards ran in seven. The side won six and drew one of their last seven matches as the season ended with a trip to Jersey and a win by 28-8 on April 29.

Mike Nicholas on the charge, & recently with fellow 'ex-Aberavon' RL stars.

Overall it was P 44, W 24, D 5, L 15 and Aberavon finished sixth in the table. Martin, Shell, flanker Ogwen Alexander and Malcolm Swain had been in the Wales B side that beat France 35-6 at Cardiff, with Martin scoring a try.

Wales toured Canada in the summer of 1973, both Martin and Shell appearing in a 76-6 win over Alberta in which Martin scored 28 points (8 cons, 4 pens) and Shell a try. Martin kicked 16 points against Quebec Maritimes and Shell played in the 79-0 win over Ontario. He was also to meet, and later marry a Canadian lady.

The ship had certainly been steadied, and with Morton Howells again captaining in 1973-74, Aberavon moved up to fifth in the Championship as well as reaching the final of the Cup. He was now aged 32 and in his ninth season at the club he has served so devotedly.

Phil Morgan took over from Max Wiltshire as coach and Allan Martin smashed the club record with 285 points while David ('The Poacher') Condon scored 17 tries in 21 appearances. In club games Aberavon beat Cardiff 8-0 and in the last four weeks of the season defeated Neath by 46-8 home and 17-14 away. In the former game, Alexander scored three of the seven tries and Martin kicked seven goals.

Into the team came 5'3" full back and Glamorgan cricketer Kim Davies from Vardre, pictured here sitting on the lap of the 'Mother of all Mothers' and supporter of all supporters, Billy's mother Mrs Evelyn Mainwaring – of whom more in our appendices. It was a season when Aberavon was the only Welsh club to win at Stradey Park, but when Ray Wilkins joined the club's ever-lengthening trail to Rugby League.

Mrs. Mainwaring, her boy and her boys, early 1970s.

Martin played in Barbarians' victories at Penarth and Newport and Ian Hall led the Welsh Police to victory over the English and was capped against Scotland, Ireland and France with Martin making his debut against Australia and appearing against Scotland and Ireland while Clive Shell emerged briefly from Edwards' giant shadow to earn that richly-deserved cap in the last two minutes against Australia.

He and Martin played in a Wales XV against Japan; Shell in the B side that defeated France B; Hall, C. Beynon (wing), John Bevan, Shell and Martin for West Glamorgan against Japan; Howells for the Western Counties against Japan and Shell (capt.) and Ogwen Alexander (try) for West Wales against Australia at Aberavon. For the Barbarians, Martin and Shell played against Moseley, Martin against Leicester and Hall (at full back) at Newport.

Clive Shell with that single cap, 1973.

The cup round wins came over Pyle 12-0, Cardiff College of Education 19-9

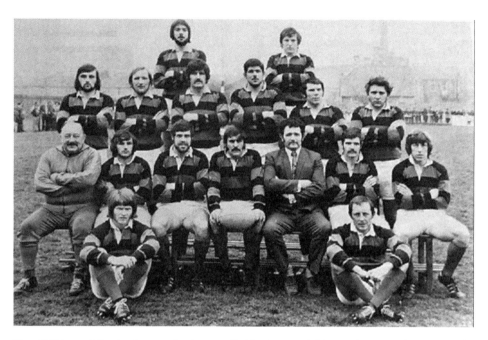

The 1984 semi-final winners. Back row: Keith Evans, Richie Davies. Standing: Malcolm Triggs, Ogwen Alexander, Billy Mainwaring, Allan Martin, Jim Owen, Clive Williams. Seated: John Griffiths (trainer), Kim Davies, Ian Hall, Morton Howells (capt.), Phil Morgan (coach), Alan Rees, Malcolm Swain. Front: John Bevan, Clive Shell.

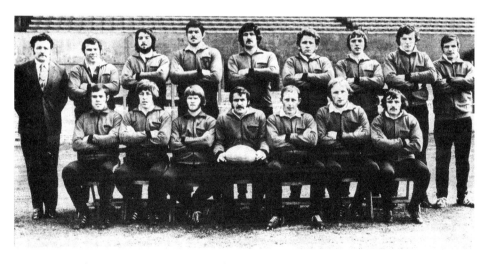

Beaten semi-finalists. Standing (left to right): Phil Morgan (coach), Jim Owen, K. Evans, Allan Martin, Billy Mainwaring, Clive Williams, S. Roper, Richie Davies, Alan Rees. Seated: Ian Hall, Malcolm Swain, John Bevan, Morton Howells (capt.), Clive Shell, Ogwen Alexander, Kim Davies.

(away), Aberavon Quins 22-3, Kenfig Hill 33-7 (away), Beddau 32-4 and Cardiff 9-4 (Hall scored a try and Martin a conversion and pen) in the semi-final at Bridgend.

The final saw Llanelli defeat Aberavon by 12-10, though wing Steve Roper scored the only try of the match. He had won a Wales Districts cap from Cimla in 1972 against Belgium. The try came after three minutes when Shell and Bevan combined to send Roper over and it was 7-6 to the 'Wizards' at half-time. Then Kim Davies had to move to scrum half as Shell received stitches.

"That was when we lost it," said Howells. *"I am convinced that though we were on their line, if Clive had been on the field we would have scored."* Aberavon led 10-9, but Andy Hill's fourth penalty won it for Llanelli.

The losing Aberavon side was: Kim Davies; Steve Roper, Malcolm Swain, Ian Hall, Alan Rees; John Bevan, Clive Shell; Clive Williams, Morton Howells (capt.), Jim Owen, Billy Mainwaring, Allan Martin, Richie Davies, Keith Evans and Ogwen Alexander.

For Swain it was the double of the English and Welsh finals, while seven of the side had won, or were to win, caps – including the strong prop Clive Williams. Overall the season's statistics were: P 35, W 24, D 0, L 11.

Morton Howells led the club for the fourth and final time in a very pleasing 1974-75 for Aberavon. They reached the Cup final again and the early season saw 13 successive wins, including Cardiff, Bristol, Bath (away) and Neath (away). Their only home defeat of the season was on April 12 when Pontypool went away 18-7 victors.

The Cup run brought victories over Glynneath (28-3 away); Cefn Cribbwr (34-0); Newbridge (15-0); Abertillery (12-6 away) and Pontypridd (10-9) in a semi-final at Cardiff won by a Steve Roper try and two Martin penalties. In the final at Cardiff on April 26, Llanelli defeated Aberavon 15-6 despite two penalties by centre Greg Rees, a

1974 & 1975 Cup Final Programmes & Ticket.

Wales Secondary Schools cap and captain of UCW, Aberystwyth recruited from Porthcawl.

John Bevan and Ian Hall were out with injury and the team, 11 of whom played in the 1974 final, was: Kim Davies; Steve Roper, Jeff Thomas, Greg Rees, David Condon; Alan Rees, Clive Shell; Clive Williams, Morton Howells (capt), Jim Owen, Allan Martin, Billy Mainwaring, Richie Davies, Phil Clarke and Ogwen Alexander. The reserves were Robert Stephens (a 1970 Wales Youth cap from Cwmavon) and Phil Bell (a Wales Boys' Club cap from Blaengarw).

Allan Martin was top scorer with 221 points, and although 'Pooler' topped the Championship, Aberavon, in second, registered a 6-6 draw at Pontypool Park. The season brought a record reading: P 38, W 26, D 3, L 9 and Bevan and Martin were capped against France, England and Scotland. Martin also appeared against Ireland, and Martin, Bevan (try) and Hall (rep.) for a Wales XV against Tonga in Cardiff, when Shell was selected but withdrew with a rib injury.

Hall suffered a compound fracture of his leg for a 'Wales XV' against NZ in that strange midweek November clash, lost 3-12 at Cardiff, when Bevan played as a replacement; Bevan and Alexander played for Wales B against France B; Hall (try), Martin and Alexander for West Wales against Tonga at Swansea and Bevan was fly half for the Barbarians against NZ

Aberavon's Welsh internationals and Barbarians, 1975:
(left to right): John Bevan, Clive Shell, Ian Hall, Billy Mainwaring, Allan Martin.

83

at Twickenham, while Shell (capt) and Martin played for the Barbarians against East Midlands.

Chris O'Callaghan, a former under-15 cap from St Joseph's Comprehensive (Port Talbot) gained Welsh Secondary Schools caps against England and France. He was to cast a few spells in his time, including at Aberavon, where small red representations of 'Wizards' were now adorning the tops of the rugby posts, and it was from the mid-1970s that a figure of a wizard featured as the emblem on the club's jerseys.

One old theory had the nickname based on the fact that many workers had come to Port Talbot from the Carmarthen area, strongly associated with the legendary wizard, Merlin. So many of those workers lived in one street that it was named Carmarthen Row and the TAG was built nearby. Bill Taylor's 1920s dubbing of 'The Wizards' seems much more likely, though!

It is hard to believe that a season in which Cardiff were beaten away in the Cup and 21-9 at home later, and when Neath were beaten four times for the first time in club history (22-3 and 20-3 at home; 9-3 and 9-0 away), was disappointing, but 1975-76 under new captain, mechanical fitter Richie Davies, was indeed so.

It was an odd season in which an 'All Star XV' won 30-18 on February 11, while in the Cup the 'Wizards' beat Llandybie (37-10), Wrexham (34-13) and Cardiff (16-12 away) but then fell 18-24 to Swansea in a home quarter-final. Allan Martin kicked six penalties, but the 'All-Whites' landed seven penalties and a dropped goal. This was the last season in which Aberavon met Neath four times and indeed, the only time Aberavon had won all four.

An elbow injury to Bevan saw Hall return after 10 months out: he was forced to play fly half, until a further injury ended his career. Bevan and Martin were capped against Australia and Martin against England, Scotland, Ireland and France in a fine Grand Slam season.

Clive Williams and Ogwen Alexander played for Wales B; Martin for the Barbarians against Australia, Penarth and Newport; centre Greg Rees skippered the Wales Universities. Hall led Crawshay's to Berlin in November; Martin toured with Wales to Japan in September, playing in four of the five matches, including another two of those 'non-cap' matches against Japan.

Williams played in Glamorgan's 18-51 loss to Australia at Neath and Martin, Swain and Bevan (capt.) for a WRU President's XV against Pontypridd, while Aberavon opened a new dressing room complex as behind the scenes club secretary Gwilym Treharne, chairman Brian Tashara and treasurer Cliff David beavered away.

Overall it ended: P 40, W 20, D 0, L 20, symmetrical if nothing else, under Phil Morgan as coach, and with Allan Martin scoring 163 points.

1974 & 1975 Cup Programmes v Cefn Cribbwr & Llandybie: note inflation!

Among the new faces were Les Keen (wing), Billy James (former under-15 and Youth cap at hooker) and John Richardson (prop), all of whom were to become full internationals.

In February, as a grand prelude to the Centenary Season to follow, Bryn Thomas (Carlton)'s networking and organizational skills had laid a spectacular 'Salute to Rugby' before a star-studded audience at the Afan Lido, 'jewel' of the seafront and (along with the endless beach), home for many years to the Welsh Squad's Sunday and other pre-international training sessions.

Clive Shell had become captain for Aberavon's 1976-77 Centenary Season, and to celebrate they met Argentina on October 6, losing 6-18, but they defeated Italy 13-4 on November 1 and in between beat a WRU President's XV 9-0 and also downed Crawshay's by 30-19.

The Argentine game saw John Bevan floored with several late tackles after kicking his side's six points. It led to a mass punch-up in front of a 7,000 crowd. The 'Wizards' were without Allan Martin (pinched nerve in his neck) and Bevan's misdirected kick led to the only try of the match, scored by centre Adolfo Travaglini.

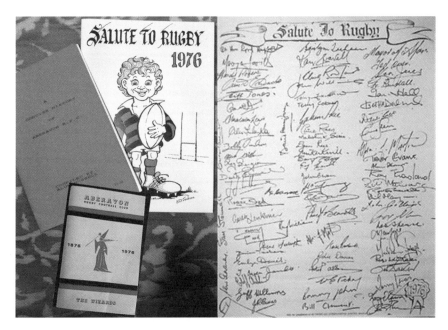

Aberavon RFC literature; and signatures from the 'Salute', 1976.

Aberavon RFC 1975-76
Back row: Robert Beresford, Les Keen, Ogwen Alexander, Phil Clarke, Ken James. Standing: Ross Richards, John Griffiths, Billy James, Brian Hancock, Clive Williams, Billy Mainwaring, Allan Martin, John Richardson, Keith Evans, Morton Howells, Phil Morgan (coach). Seated: Clive Shell, Alan Rees (vice-capt.), Cliff David (hon. treasurer), Brian Tashara (chairman), Richie Davies (capt.), Lord Heycock (president), Gwilym Treharne (hon. secretary), Jeff Thomas, John Bevan. Front: Phil Bessant, Kim Davies.

In the Italy game Steve Roper and Ogwen Alexander scored tries, Martin goaled one and Hall, who had come out of retirement, dropped a goal, while in the President's XV game, Clive Williams scored a try and Greg Rees placed a penalty and conversion.

Aberavon life member Hywel Thomas was made WRU President, but there was tragic misfortune for Shell, who suffered a broken jaw in the 15-6 Cup semi-final defeat by Cardiff at Swansea. Not one journalist suggested who helped Clive break his own jaw(!), though the *Welsh Brewers Annual* stated it was the result of a double tackle. Others, though, felt in no doubt how it happened and exactly which international player did it....

John Richardson, though, was suspended for eight weeks for being dismissed against Llanelli and a further 12 weeks after a Bridgend game, while Williams had a month's suspension after a sending-off against Pontypool.

Aberavon had beaten Dinas Powys (47-0 away), Whitland (31-0 away), Aberavon Quins (29-12) and Bridgend (10-9) before the semi-final at Swansea. With no reserve scrum half, Hall had to play there and Peter Shadis from Pyle/Kenfig Hill, came on to play in the threequarters while Brian Hancock replaced injured No 8 Keith Evans.

The game at Bedford in February was won by 19-7 and was the first meeting of the clubs since 1895. Aberavon also visited London Scottish, but lost 6-10 to a try by Scotland cap Alastair McHarg, who was opposed by Adrian Owen. A day later, on a Sunday, the side played a game at Basildon RFC in aid of Ashleigh Centre for the mentally handicapped.

Aberavon finished ninth in the Championship, with Martin scoring 144 points and Les Keen 16 tries, while two other fine wings emerged in Kevin James and track runner Jeff Griffiths. Overall, Aberavon had: P 37, W 23, D 3, L 11, Hall eventually bowing out with his final appearance against Swansea on April 16. He, Mainwaring and Howells ran out ahead of the rest of the team as it was announced that it would be the last game for all three. For Billy and Morton, all that was to change!

Martin played in all the five nations games; Clive Williams against England and Scotland, as well as for Wales B, with Alexander against France B; Martin, Bevan and Williams all toured NZ with the Lions and Martin played in a Test, as well as appearing with Bevan in the tour match against Fiji. Williams and Richie Davies played for a Combined Welsh Clubs team against Japan.

There was a big honour for hooker Morton Howells, who played for the Barbarians against both Penarth and Swansea. In the latter game French star Jean-Pierre Rives was carried off injured but said: *"C'est magnifique. I play, I sing, I laugh and I drink beer!"* Howells was the only uncapped forward in that Barbarian side.

'Chief Wizard': Aberavon's Wales lock forward Billy Mainwaring.

Chris O'Callaghan was now at Loughborough College and he scored a try in the UAU final win at Twickenham, plus a mighty penalty out of the mud against Swansea University and a try in the annual needle match against St Luke's College. He played for both Bridgend and Aberavon while on college holidays.

In May-June 1977, the club toured Barbados with Dr. Keith James as manager. They beat Barbados 82-0 at Bridgetown with Greg Rees scoring 38 points, a club record that still remains. The second match, also at Bridgetown, saw Barbados beaten by 42-3. The players did valuable local coaching work and also won a Sevens tournament. Scrum half Alun Lane (Kenfig Hill) was drafted in after the Shell injury and it is reported that Taibach fly half Rob David also made the trip.

In 1977-78, with Shell recovering from injury, he was again named captain. Ex-Youth cap Keri Coslett, younger brother of Kel, joined from Llanelli but Greg Rees moved to London Welsh. Adrian Owen was sent off against Llanelli in the second match of the season, getting a lengthy suspension that led to Billy Mainwaring coming out of retirement. Just a month later, when hooker Billy James was dismissed for stamping at home to Bedford, Morton Howells also made an unscheduled return.

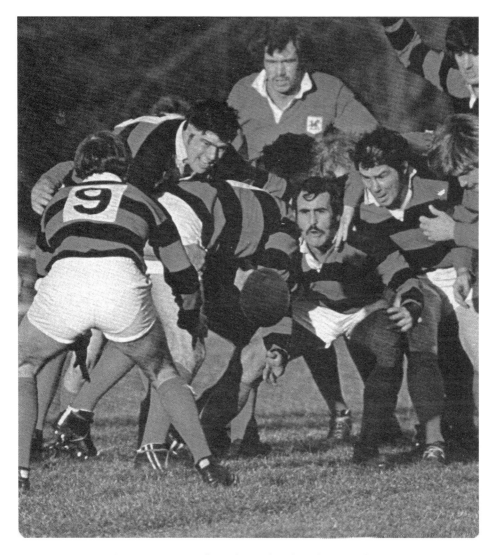

Mainwaring, Martin, Morton Howells and Co. shield Shell at London Welsh.

It was a 'curate's egg' type of season, with the team mainly better than their eventual ninth place suggests and with the best performances being in defeating Crawshay's 35-16, Neath 37-11 and Northampton 32-17.

In the Cup, Aberavon knocked out Crumlin (16-6), Ystrad Rhondda (56-10), Bridgend (10-6) and Llanelli (19-13). In the semi-final, a huge unforgettable hailstorm hit Cardiff just as the sides ran out, and Avon's hopes were washed away by two tries from Wales threequarter Gareth Evans, ensuring underdogs Newport a 10-6 win.

Aberavon fly half Keri Coslett.

In successive days in February Aberavon won 28-9 at Hampstead and 71-18 against the Bank of England, the latter being in aid of Life Education for Autistic People. Keri Coslett scored 264 points overall, including 28 points (2t, 7c, 2p) in the Cup win over Ystrad Rhondda; Greg Rees got 118, while Neil Hutchings from Treorchy (25), Jeff Griffiths (17) and Les Keen (16) were the top try-scorers. Overall, it was to finish: P 37, W 22, D 1, L 14.

Martin played in all the four games of another Welsh Grand Slam; John Richardson played for Wales B; Martin for the Barbarians against Penarth; Richardson for the Barbarians against Cardiff and Swansea but Clive Williams missed the whole season due to a knee injury.

Both Richardson and Martin made the 1978 Wales summer tour to Australia with Martin playing in both Tests and Richardson being a replacement in the second. Chris O'Callaghan skippered Loughborough College to a UAU title and M. G. Thomas (Duffryn Comp) played at prop.

In 1978-79 Clive Shell was the captain for a third successive season, but it was a disappointing one with Aberavon dreadful away from home, yet hard to beat at home. They reached the Cup semi-finals, but lost 3-6 to Pontypridd at Bridgend despite a dropped goal by Avon fly half Bernard Thomas, from Llanelli. Ponty scored the decisive try just five minutes from time.

The earlier Cup wins were over Laugharne (37-0 away), Porthcawl (15-0), Brynamman (26-10 away) and Bedwas (26-0), as the 'Wizards' sank to 14th in the table, their worst position since the Second World War. The season included a visit by a Bucharest XV, who out-muscled Aberavon by 20-7, but there were wins over Neath by 28-6 home and 22-19 away, though the hard frost 'ended' rugby for 52 successive days.

Brian Marshall from Senghenydd had become coach after Phil Morgan retired. John Bevan quit playing, while Coslett or Thomas took the fly-half spot role. Also 'gone' was Billy Mainwaring – again. New full back Wynford Lewis was player of the year, Keri Coslett scored 161 points, Les Keen 18 tries and No. 8 Phil Clarke, a garage owner from Pyle, notched 14. The year's final tallies read: P 34, W 14, D 2, L 18.

Martin, Richardson and Shell all played for West Wales against NZ and Martin for Wales and the Barbarians against them, as well as in all the five nations matches, so winning the quadruple Triple Crown. He scored a try against Ireland and a conversion against England and also played for the Barbarians against Cardiff.

Chris O'Callaghan in University action, and later....

Neil Hutchings represented the Barbarians against NZ, Leicester (try), Penarth and Newport and scored tries for Wales B against Argentine and France B. Keen played for a WRU President's XV against Bridgend and Richardson for Wales against England and the Barbarians against Cardiff and Newport (try).

Chris O'Callaghan moved on to Cambridge University, gained a Blue in a 25-7 victory over Oxford, also played against the touring All Blacks, and would be heard of more at the TAG in years to come, while Tim Fauvel and Ray Giles (both products of Cornelly) gained Youth caps. Hope for the future, then, as the club's 'Switchback Seventies' neared their close.

8

1979-1989

Tricky times ahead.....

If the UK had lived through a so-called 'Winter of Discontent' in the late 1970s, then 'Avon fans were to endure several such in sporting terms over the decade that followed. The 'Merit Table' of first-class clubs had grown to 18 by the 60s, then 19 in the 70s, and in these 1980s the Talbot boys were only to finish in the top half four times.

Hooker Billy James became captain for 1979-80 but the 'Wizards' slipped to ninth in the Championship, having lost Neil Hutchings to Cardiff, Clive Williams to Swansea (further caps) and Jeff Griffiths to Llanelli (non-cap try-scorer v Romania in October). Allan Martin played five games for Llanelli then returned to Aberavon.

Some topsy-turvy results included conceding 10 tries in a 3-54 loss at Bristol, being what the *Times* newspaper called *'a raggle-taggle bunch'*. There was also a first-ever Round One defeat in the Cup, losing 0-9 home

Capped from Aberavon and Swansea, Wales and Lions prop Clive Williams

to Maesteg, but wins included all three meetings with Neath (two at the Gnoll) and 29-22 home to Cardiff, before April brought seven successive losses, conceding 166 points.

San Isidro (Argentina) were beaten 19-18, but Aberavon lost 22-40 to an International XV in aid of the Barrie Lewis Memorial Fund, after the club prop and his wife died tragically in a road accident.

Overall the record added up to: P 45, W 22, D 3, L 20. Wynford Lewis scored 161 points (including 15 tries) and Martyn Thomas also notched 15. Martin and Les Keen played for Wales in all the five-nations games, with Les scoring a good try against Scotland.

"I was given the ball with a half-gap," said the modest Keen. *"I handed off my opposite number Keith*

Les Keen scores for Wales against Scotland, 1980.

Robertson with my right hand, tucked the ball under my left arm and raced as fast as I could to the corner with Andy Irvine chasing me."

Keen played for Wales B; John Richardson (capt.), Clive Shell, Martin and Keen (2 tries) for West Wales against Romania; Richardson (capt.) and James for the WRU Presidents XV against Ebbw Vale; James and Wynford Lewis were on the Wales tour of USA/Canada in 1980 with James playing against USA, and Martin and Clive Williams (now Swansea) toured with the Lions to South Africa.

A new star was scrum half Ray Giles, who had led Wales Youth to South Africa and a 30-25 Test win. Chris O'Callaghan played for the Barbarians, English Universities (capt.), British Universities, UAU (capt.), Public School Wanderers and, even, Neath! He also played for Cambridge University against Portugal in 1979 and Japan at Tokyo in 1980.

Before 1980-81 had started Clive Shell had retired and young Ray Giles stepped in at scrum half with Omri Jones as coach, John Bevan his assistant and Billy James again captain. The terracing at the ground was given a facelift, too, and the club's pack included Paul Knight, Adrian Owen, brothers John and Chris O'Callaghan and Mike Edwards, with Gary Matthews splendid at centre.

Chris O'Callaghan commented: *"I always remember those midweek matches when everyone went down with an attack of 'Gwent Flu', particularly when playing*

Billy James and Clive Shell take on old rivals Llanelli.

Pontypool away! I loved those games and never missed one. They were bare-knuckle fights where you gave no quarter and asked for none. I used to get up the next morning, with my face looking like the Michelin road map of France and when I

looked in the mirror, I didn't want to see my reflection. I just wanted to know that I was still alive!"

September's highlight was an 18-0 win over Cardiff and October saw an 18-17 win at Pontypool Park that took Pooler's 18-month-old ground record. James, Les Keen and Allan Martin did not play, but Owen led with O'Callaghan revelling in the forward duel. Overall it was 22 losses and one draw before the 'Wizards' next won there in October 2005.

December brought a 6-6 draw on Boxing Day at home to Neath, then February saw a win over Irish club Palmerston by 12-3 and a Cup quarter-final loss by 9-17 at Bridgend. Earlier Cup wins had come over Senghenydd (14-3 away) and Pontypool Utd (20-6 away). Aberavon ended with

Omri 'Om the Bomb' Jones.

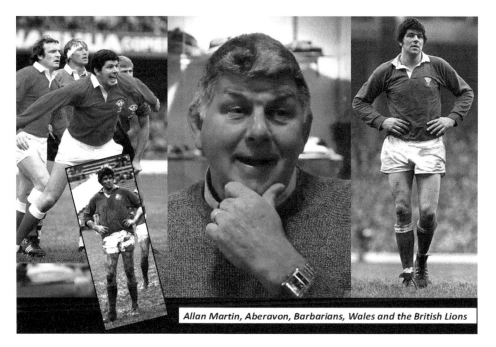

Allan Martin, Aberavon, Barbarians, Wales and the British Lions

away losses at Neath, Swansea and Bridgend, the totals amounting to: P 38, W 22, D 3, L 13.

The side was seventh in the table with fly half Mike Lewis (Cwmllynfell) scoring 199 points and Bernard Thomas 157, while wing Paul Bamsey gained 13 tries. Allan Martin's long and distinguished international career ended on 34 caps after playing against NZ in 1980 and Ireland and France in 1981. He also appeared for Wales against a WRU President's World XV.

Aberavon toured British Columbia in August 1981 and beat Burnaby 51-0 with nine tries and Fraser Valley 17-9. Next was a 16-3 win over James Bay (the 7-time BC champions in 8 years) at Victoria and a 22-22 draw with Vancouver Reps. John O'Callaghan replaced his brother Chris, who was on honeymoon, while Omri Jones was coach and Frank Williams tour manager.

Allan Martin took the captaincy for 1981-82 in a season of good wins and bad losses which ended with eighth position in the Championship. John Bevan had taken over from Omri Jones as head coach, meaning a bigger accent on back play, and among those used were Andy Martin and Mike Carrington, the latter joining Neath and then St Helen's RL in 1988. The pack included the powerful Adrian Owen and Jeff Jenkins.

The season began with skipper Martin sent off against Llanelli and suspended for a month, but Aberavon won 25-11 at Cardiff, demolished Bath 46-9 and won 27-14 at Northampton. December saw a defeat away to London Welsh (4-21) then a 6-0 win at Neath on Boxing Day. January brought a home loss to Cardiff (6-12) before a splendid 25-10 Cup success at Pontypridd, with earlier Cup wins over Aberavon Quins (12-4) and Whitland (25-3).

The game against Cardiff in January evokes memories for Paul Williams. *"I recall that it was on a Thursday evening in sub-zero temperatures. Ken Rowlands was referee and several times during the second half he stamped on parts of the pitch to see if it had frozen solid. Half an hour after the final whistle it was snowing heavily. By the following morning the whole area was at a standstill. Other than main roads, which were cleared by snow-ploughs, everywhere was under several feet of snow. Our car was buried under a five-foot snowdrift".*

A Romanian side were beaten 14-10 in a February that also saw an 18-0 Cup win at Newport. Nine wins in a row ended with an unlucky semi-final loss by 6-9 to Bridgend at Swansea. The media saw Aberavon as the better side and Gerald Davies (*The Times*) stated that Mike Lewis had scored the try of the season. Coslett converted, but Gary Pearce placed two penalties and a drop goal to win it.

The semi-final side was: Keri Coslett; Martyn Thomas, Gary Matthews, Colin Lewis, Kevin James; Mike Lewis, Ray Giles; Paul Knight, Billy James (rep: Kevin Helt), Steve Hopkin, Allan Martin (capt.), Adrian Owen, Steve Thomas, Jeff Jenkins, Mike Edwards.

Mike Lewis scored 186 points, forming a good half-back combination with Giles, while Bernard Thomas returned to Llanelli. Martyn Thomas scored 22 tries and was close to Welsh selection while young Kevin James

Not quite enough: Cup semi-final v Bridgend, 1982.

from Cwmllynfell was a splendid wing. Flanker Steve Thomas notched 14 tries and Keri Coslett scored 97 points.

A disastrous end of season, though, included a 3-21 Easter home loss to Neath and overall it was P 36, W18, D 2, L 16 as Martin again left, this time to live and play in South Africa, though he soon returned. He had played for West Wales against Australia at Llanelli along with Knight, Owen, Lewis, (Martyn) Thomas and Giles (rep) with the latter leading Wales B against Australia. In the National Sevens at Aberavon, the 'Wizards' beat Neath 14-4 in a semi-final, but lost the final 14-24 to South Glamorgan Institute.

Adrian Owen became captain for 1982-83 and while the club dropped to 11th in the table and took a thrashing from the Maoris, they won the Bridgend and Rovigo Sevens titles – the invitation to the latter coming via Roy Bish, who returned to coach Aberavon after six years in Italy. The previous club coach, John Bevan, was now in charge of Wales.

Billy James

Aberavon   5ft 10ins
Hooker   13st

WELSH RUGBY UNION SQUAD MEMBER 81-82

Hooker Billy James, in the Welsh Squad of 1982.

Mike Lewis set a club record of 306 points and tries came from Kevin James (23) and Ray Giles (15). Billy James played for Wales against the Maoris before winning caps in all the Five-Nation games. He and Giles toured with Wales to Spain and both appeared in the 'Test'. Billy also played for the Barbarians against East Midlands, Penarth and Swansea and with Kevin xJames for Wales B; Andy Martin played for Wales Students while skipper Owen was sent off (again) against Llanelli.

A 34-18 win over the Mayor of Afan's Select XV began the season, but performances were poor until a 33-10 win at Northampton just three days before Aberavon met the Maoris, who ran riot with six tries in a 34-6 scoreline with All Black centre Stephen Pokere outstanding.

Coach Bish stated: *"You can't keep on tackling and tackling against the quality of attack that the Maoris unleashed. They outplayed us for possession and our forwards knew they were beaten."*

Locks Martin and Owen had no answer and Aberavon were run ragged, with one try starting on the Maoris goal-line before their wing Mike Clamp

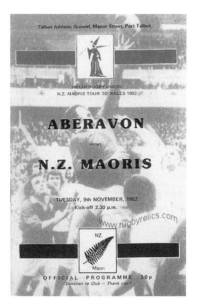

Aberavon v the Maoris programme, 1982.

touched down at the other end. He bagged a hat-trick and Pokere a brace, while Mike Lewis kicked two home penalties.

There was a 39-23 win away to London Welsh and Neath were beaten 15-10 on Boxing Day. The latter, though, were the club's Cup opponents for the first-ever time on January 22 and they won 27-20. Earlier rounds saw wins over Ruthin (39-4) and Neath Athletic (19-9 away).

April brought victories over London Welsh (29-9), Llanelli (31-19) and by 15-12 at Neath, before a midweek visit to West Germany saw verdicts over the 21st Royal Engineers (30-4) and RAF Gutersloh (70-4). Overall, there was a record of: P 36, W 19, D 1, L 16.

The Bridgend Sevens were won, with Andy Martin 'Man of the Tournament' and victory also came in the Rovigo Tornament, with successes including those over Cardiff (26-14) and Moseley (36-12) from a team of: Andy Martin, Martyn Thomas (capt), Andrew Jones, Gary Matthews, Steve Thomas, Tim Fauvel and Paul Marley.

Adrian Owen came on for Marley in the final, when Neath's Wales cap Alan Edmunds also 'guested' to replace Andy Martin. Fauvel was 'Man of the Tournament', while David Beaton was the Chairman of the Supporters club during its 50th anniversary, with Harry Woodhouse as secretary and Harry Harris as treasurer.

Adrian Owen continued as captain in 1983-84 with Roy Bish coach, and a 'middling' campaign followed. September brought the visit of Bayonne, who won 13-4 and in November the 'Wizards' just scraped past Nantyffyllon 10-9 in the Cup, forwards coach Jim Owen having lasted 28 minutes before being sent off.

December included a draw at London Welsh and a 31-7 win at the Gnoll. Pontypridd were knocked out of the Cup 18-3 after Aberavon's previous round win over Tenby Utd (35-3 away). Ebbw Vale were beaten 16-7 away in a quarter-final, but the semi-final against Neath at Bridgend was a poor affair, with a 4-1 penalty-count putting Neath through by 12-3.

Paul Williams said: "An 8-0 home win over Ebbw Vale with two tries by prop David Joseph was followed 10 days later by a Cup tie on an even colder afternoon at Eugene Cross Park (it started snowing as we arrived). Jonathan Griffiths scored a try and early on Ebbw lock John Williams was sent off for stamping. Five minutes later Joseph followed for a similar offence. The remainder of the match was a blur... a bit like the steadily falling snow."

36-years-young Allan Martin and Les Keen were still playing, with Mike Lewis scoring 201 points and Andrew Jones 143. Kevin James scored 12 tries and Ray Giles 10 as a campaign of many away losses saw the side stay 11th in the table with a symmetrical record: P 38, W 18, D 2, L 18.

Scrum half Ray Giles plays – and scores – for Wales v Japan.

Chris O'Callaghan led Crawshay's against a WRU President's World XV at Llanelli; Andy Martin gained a Cambridge Blue; Billy James was capped against Romania and Scotland and Giles against Romania. Both James and Giles played in the non-cap match against Japan and Neville Walsh continued as Crawshay's team manager (1977-1987).

Sadly, season 1984-85 saw Aberavon at its least successful to that date in post-war years, finishing 15th in the 'Championship'. Adrian Owen moved to Bridgend, leaving Billy James to return as captain. Jim Owen's coaching job went to Clive Shell, Mike Lewis transferred to Newport and Les Keen, scorer of 101 tries, went into semi-retirement.

Paul Williams said: *"Wing Kevin James' defection to Rugby League came as a complete surprise – he was one of the best wings in Wales, but though he played for Wales B, he declined a call-up to the Welsh squad because he was 'too busy building his house' and working as a policeman, so it was surprising that he played for Hull RL as 'A Trialist' and scored two tries, joining them in October and then scored a try in the Cup final at Wembley. He'd won the Aberavon Supporters 'Player of the Year' for 1982-83 and wrote thanking them and apologising for the clandestine manner of his departure."*

Paul Yardley and Tim Fauvel did good work in the back row and full back, Andy Martin, followed his Blue for Cambridge in the 1983 Varsity match with a further appearance in December, this time as a wing.

Billy James was capped in all the five-nations matches and for the Barbarians against Cardiff and Swansea. Among good new faces were Chris

Bradshaw and Richard Diplock, with Hugh Morris, later a Glamorgan and England cricketer and administrator, a fly half from South Glamorgan Institute.

In the Cup, after defeating Blaenau Gwent (39-3) and Tenby Utd (14-9), came a resounding 0-25 home loss to Pontypool with Jeff Jenkins sent off. The home ground was no longer a fortress and away form was again poor, with 37 points conceded at Bath, 42 at Swansea and 45 at Cardiff: yet the 'Wizards' won at Bridgend (21-9) for the first time in seven years. Andrew Jones scored 171 points while Ray Giles ran in 15 tries and Peter Jones (from Maesteg) 14. Overall the stats story read: P 40, W 16, D 0, L 24.

The season ended with a trip to Barcelona in May, defeating Catalan Select 32-13 and then scoring 11 tries in a 48-4 win over Gerona Select, in which Yardley and Diplock scored three apiece. Crawshay's toured South Africa in 1985, much against the wishes of many, but included Allan Martin (capt.), Mike Lewis, Ray Giles and Jeff Jenkins with Neville Walsh as manager.

The 1985-86 season saw captain Ray Giles in outstanding form and he skippered Wales B on tour to play Italy B and Italy A with lock Ian ('Billy') Brown also appearing in both games. Giles led a President's XV against London Welsh at Twickenham; played for a Merit Table XV at Cross Keys; won a cap as a replacement at home to Fiji (Billy James also played) and scored 16 tries, helping Aberavon to sixth in the Championship. The season brought 20 wins in 35 matches.

Former prop Cliff David was now the treasurer and Bill Lewis the secretary, while the club coach was Richie Davies, aided by Keri Coslett, as Allan Martin and Les Keen had joined Penarth. However, Mike Lewis, whose moves to Newport and then Lazio had been due to his losing his job in the miner's strike, had returned and scored 112 points – and over 1,000 in his club career – forming a splendid partnership with Giles.

Richard Diplock scored 13 tries and Billy James won caps in all the five-nation games and against Fiji, Tonga and Western Samoa on a tour from which Tim Fauvel pulled out with injury after selection. The Cup saw away wins over Narberth (14-0) and Aberavon Quins (36-9), before victory at Llanelli (whom Aberavon beat three times) by 11-10 in a quarter-final.

Paul Williams stated: *"Richard Diplock scored a try and Lewis kicked a penalty but Llanelli led 10-7 late on and scrum-half Jonathan Griffiths broke up the touchline, but his inside pass was intercepted by Giles, who turned on his heel, broke away, kicked over Martin Gravelle's head and regathered to score in the corner. It was only the second-ever home cup loss for Llanelli."*

The 'Wizards' took Bath's unbeaten record by 16-15 and scored 25 points against Bristol and 24 against Cardiff, also winning a Spanish tour match in May against Valencia (54-12) after a game against Elche had been

Aberavon 1986-87, captained by Ray Giles. Coach Richie Davies is standing on right.

cancelled. The on-field loss hardest to take was by 6-15 to Newport in the Cup semi-final, but the biggest tragedy was the death of John Bevan, who had resigned his Wales coaching job in November due to the cancer to which he succumbed on June 5, 1986.

In his late-eighties volume on *The Rugby Clubs of Wales* the late David Parry-Jones, of BBC Wales and beyond, commented kindly on the club all the way from the early days: '*God created Rugby to save the dreaded Bascombe brothers from the gallows'* – to that 1986 quarter final: '*unflinching resistance.... marvellous Giles try unforgettable victory....*'

However, he also knew of the aftermath: '*But Aberavon were running out of steam. The semi-final brought defeat by Newport, and the onset of the Troubles, which were to prove chronic.*'

For the moment, though, the club looked to bounce back and Ray Giles continued as captain in 1986-87.

Unfortunately, the campaign was to see another new low since WW2, as the club finished 16th, failing dismally away and achieving little at home. David Joseph and Jonathan Griffiths went to Neath, Jeff Jenkins to Bridgend and Ian Brown to Swansea while 38-yr-old Allan Martin returned from Penarth.

Ray Giles, Barbarian.

An International XV won 50-18 in September 17th's match to celebrate 100 years since the club had joining the WRU, and in December the club lost at home to Newport for the first time in 15 years. The final two matches, both away, brought losses at Neath (10-48) and Pontypool (15-51). Overall it was sad reading: P 38, W 13, D 0, L 25.

In the Cup the 'Wizards' beat Tumble (26-0) and, despite changing in an old chapel, 34-3 at Cwmtillery, but lost at Pontypool (0-25). Among the new faces was Simon King, a student who scored a try against Northampton over Easter, while Mike Lewis scored 287 points and Stephen Jones 102 with wing Peter Jones (Maesteg) and Ray Giles both scoring 11 tries.

On the sunnier side, loyal Billy James was capped by Wales against England, Scotland and Ireland, in that last game becoming the only Aberavon player ever to skipper Wales. It also proved to be his last as, although he was selected for the 1987 World Cup, he was injured in training at Wellington and flown home.

Giles was called up to the World Cup when Llanelli's Jonathan Griffiths withdrew and was capped against Canada – his last international appearance. He also played for the Barbarians against East Midlands. Wales prop Ian Stephens (Bridgend) made one appearance for Aberavon.

On a longer-term recruit, Paul Williams commented: *"Kevin George from Llangennech was initially recruited to cover full-back and scrum-half roles. But, he proved an unqualified success at centre and he went on to forge a superb midfield partnership with Jon Jardine in subsequent seasons."*

It was around this time that the Oriel Gallery in Cardiff held a visual celebration of the 'first-class' club game in Wales, with an accompanying booklet containing a potted history and comments on each such outfit. (At least Aberavon were always first alphabetically in such lists!) That for the Wizards concluded: *'Their squad is invariably given a 'promising' tag, but they have rarely managed recently to achieve any real consistency. On their day, they are capable of playing rugby a swell as any...'* Hard to argue?

Time moves on, of course, and change: but thirty years on there is a heavy irony in reading Barry John's foreword to the publication mentioned: even 20 years ago, the warning bells were ringing, but not in 1986 when he confidently asserted: *'The universal envy of the likes of Mike Gibson, Gordon Brown and David Duckham is the Welsh Club structure, and the intensity of the rivalry.*

They envy our 8,000 to 12,000 crowds, games full of passion, enlightened knowledgeable followers and an 'unfair' advantage for international readiness, hardened both mentally and physically by our schedules for the demands of Test Rugby. Cardiff helped John Scott – and hence England!'

Tradition is an integral part of Welsh Rugby and every one of the 'senior' Welsh clubs has contributed to its drama and development in its own, often different way...'

Billy James, the only Aberavon player to captain Wales.

Aberavon RFC has certainly done that, but often with the drama – or melodrama – off the field, and few were to see more graphically at first hand the trials, tribulations and unfortunate timing of the arrival of professional rugby and the effects of the efforts – often contradictory and counter-productive – of the authorities to codify and administer it. Sometimes the club may not have helped themselves, too, but the world described by Barry John was to prove a universe away by 2000, let alone 2015 – and who knows how the picture will look in 2020?

Back in 1987-88, though, a new full back emerged in Lyndon Lewis from Gorseinon, who had played three times the previous season, though on his debut he had dislocated his shoulder against Llanelli. Also breaking through were back-row forwards Nigel Spender (Taibach), Colin Roberts (Glyncorrwg/ Wales Districts), and Gerald Williams. Jim Owen returned as coach and John Richardson team manager,

Wales prop John Richardson: & also with John Bevan as subs in Paris, 1977.

ABERAVON
Rugby Football Club
"The Wizards"

JOHN BEVAN
MEMORIAL MATCH

ABERAVON and NEATH
v.
A WELSH INTERNATIONAL XV

TALBOT ATHLETIC GROUND
Wednesday,
September 9th, 1987

Official 50p Programme

Donation to John Bevan Appeal Fund

The John Bevan Memorial Match, 1987.

while Gary Matthews passed 250 appearances.

Skipper Ray Giles though, was to quit after disagreeing with Richardson and joined Cardiff and Billy James took over in another season of struggle which led to big trouble. Indeed, over the next two years, with players, management, committee and the WRU, it might be said that there was more going on behind the scenes than at a dodgy pantomime: but sadly, it wasn't funny.

Before all that, September saw Aberavon/Neath lose 8-34 to a Wales International XV in a John Bevan Memorial match at Aberavon and then the 'Wizards' had a fine 15-12 win at Cardiff. Paul Williams said: *"A poor game saw Cardiff lead 12-3 with only a couple of minutes left to play, when Nigel Spender drove over and the conversion succeeded. Cardiff restarted to wing Edward Ellis, who ran to halfway, kicked infield and Gary Matthews chased, hacked on, regathered and scored."*

Having had Nigel Spender sent off against Penarth and both Jeff Jenkins and Leighton Gerrard four days later against Bridgend, the WRU issued a warning to the club with Jenkins banned for 20 weeks. In response, club secretary Tony John said: *"We are not a bunch of thugs. We play hard rugby within the rules."*

Cup wins over Bridgend Sports Club (25-3 away) and Carmarthen Ath (17-6), were followed by defeat at Cardiff and John O'Callaghan sent off, but there was a Cup win at Pontypridd thanks to the boot of Mike Lewis and an interception try by Gary Matthews.

Llanharan were beaten 20-14 away, though the semi-final at Swansea saw the 'Wizards' take a 0-38 pasting from Llanelli. April saw wins by 51-0 over Northampton and 23-4 against London Welsh, but the last seven matches brought five losses, including Neath (6-24) at home and Llanelli (3-46) away. The club finished 12th, despite Mike Lewis providing 272 points. Gerald Williams scored nine tries, the final tallies read: P 38, W 16, D 4, L 18, but the most crucial statistic was this next one.

Paul Williams commented: *"When Karl Yates became the fifth player to be sent off, it earned a two-week ban for the entire squad. It was the first of several hammer blows that saw the club in turmoil through the close-season with a major falling-out between the players and committee, culminating in 18 players, including skipper Billy James, who joined Swansea, parting company with Aberavon.*

Issues of finance, tactical priorities and the way forward have been suggested as amongst the reasons for the dissension. Williams: *"The long-term effects that saw the club having to rebuild a squad from scratch inevitably led to a series of very poor seasons, and when leagues were introduced two years later the WRU approach of grading teams according to their results over the previous three years took its toll with Aberavon condemned to the second tier."*

Meanwhile Tim Fauvel became the last-ever Welsh cap directly from Aberavon as he toured New Zealand in the summer of 1988, playing against Waikato, Wellington, Hawke's Bay and Taranaki, before gaining his cap as a replacement in the 1st Test. He also appeared as a replacement for a Rest of Wales XV against Cardiff and John Jardine, Gary Richardson and Gerald Williams

Tim Fauvel, last-ever Welsh cap direct from Aberavon.

all played for Central Glamorgan Under-21s, who lost 0-21 to their NZ equivalents at the TAG.

One man already a 'fixture' at the club was David (Dai) Beaton, with the backroom staff and as an occasional touch-judge and he was still serving Aberavon well in 2017. However, more than a whole team had left by 1988-89, including John Richardson and Jim Owen. After starting as captain, and after 14 years' service, Billy James had departed reluctantly and with a diplomatic silence, while Mike Lewis went to London Welsh, Richard Diplock to Bridgend (where he won a cap) and the O'Callaghan brothers joined Aberavon Quins.

The 1988-89 season started two weeks late due to the WRU suspension, but while only two games were played in September and both lost, nine were crammed into October. During the season 31 matches were lost, including four in a row which conceded 181 points. It ended with nine defeats and one win (Briton Ferry 50-6 away) in the final 10 matches.

Defeats included 10-34 and 6-42 to Neath and 6-66 at home to Llanelli, but the worst was by 6-19 in the Cup, away to none other than Aberavon Quins, for whom Chris O'Callaghan was a try-scorer. This came after an earlier win at Senghenydd (16-9).

Paul Williams: *"The ultimate indignity of that season was the defeat by Aberavon Quins, as the presence of John and Chris O'Callaghan alone was too much for some of the less experienced members of the pack, who folded meekly at the slightest hint of intimidation, an art at which the brothers were past masters! It was the first time for the club to lose a cup-tie to a 'second-class club' as those outside the Merit Table were known back then. It wasn't the last, though!"*

Allan Martin and Les Keen had returned as coaches along with Richie Davies and Neville Walsh was the team manager, while the loyal Gary Matthews became captain and was splendid at centre. However, the club sank down the table and on January 21 could not raise a team to play Bristol.

The one bright side was a surprising and well-deserved 21-11 win over tourists Western Samoa, with tries coming from John Hopkins, Middleton, Andrew Jones and replacement Forester. Full back Lyndon Lewis kicked five points.

The Wizards played with passion and purpose and coach Martin admitted: *"I feared the worst, but the team responded beyond anything we imagined."* Neville Walsh added: *"I did not think we could win, but there was an unquenchable spirit in all our players."* John Billot called Lewis *"a player of vision and admirable decision, who steadied the defence and strengthened the attack."*

The sad facts at the end of the turbulent campaign confirmed a new statistical low, as Aberavon ended 16th in the 'Merit Table': P 40, W 10, D 1, L 29. Neil Forester was top scorer with 95 points and nine tries each were scored by Phil Middleton and wing Hopkins.

Middleton played for Wales under-21s and Adrian Varney for Crawshay's in Moscow. Was there hope for the future? Paul Williams said: *"Andrew Jones started the season on a wing, but moved to fly-half where he partnered Neville Roberts, who spent the entire season working minor miracles behind a pack that was constantly retreating.*

"The 6-66 loss to Llanelli saw the 'Wizards' start without a hooker. Adrian Varney was pressed into service, so it was not surprising that it didn't end well! He joined from Cardigan and would run all day and give penalties away for even longer. He moved to Neath the following season.

"For the opening match, players had been introduced to one another in the dressing room before taking the field. The dismal playing record that season doesn't do justice to the hard work Neville Walsh and the coaches put in to try and strengthen the squad – no easy task, as the club's reputation was at an all-time low following the pre-season turmoil."

As the Eighties neared their end, then, the only way was – hopefully – up, but David Parry Jones was not too far out when he wrote in 1989: *'Neville Walsh, now departed from his role, had faced an uphill battle to unite the club, quell internecine disputes and recreate in the players loyalty and purpose. His man-management was the key to bringing calm and some of the old Wizardry back to the Talbot Athletic Ground: but Aberavon's full recovery threatens to be long and agonizing....'*

9

1989-1999:

The Ups – and Downs – of the Leagues.....

It has become infuriatingly familiar for TV wannabees and others to use the phrase 'It's been an emotional roller-coaster'. We would of course never stoop to such a cliché, but let's say Aberavon's 'journey'(?) through the League labyrinth of the 90s did indeed resemble somewhat a visit to the Barry Island Scenic Railway or Porthcawl's Water Chute. And rather like Ruth Jones (Aberavon, TV and the World) they could often have turned to the WRU and asked *'What's occurrin'?......*

The 1989-90 season was the last before leagues began and Aberavon fell to 17th in the Championship. Centre Gary Matthews continued to lead, but coach Allan Martin was sacked in December and Max Wiltshire took over, with Les Keen as backs coach.

The club lost Tim Fauvel, who was working in Australia and playing for Wollongong. Yet, despite defeat after defeat Aberavon astonishingly reached the semi-final of the Cup. Martin said: *"I feel a victim of circumstances. The club is only worried about finishing in the top half of the 'Merit Table', so that it can begin in the top division of next season's league."*

Phil Sutton scored 185 points and Gwilym Wilkins 11 tries, but for 'Avon it was to be the end of players capped and of playing touring sides, and bigger changes in the rugby world were to be on the horizon. So, Aberavon began with a home loss to Glamorgan Wanderers (who completed the double) and lost another 36 games, including 0-50 at Neath on Boxing Day.

The Cup began with a 30-9 win at Carmarthen Quins, then 13-3 against Laugharne a week after Martin's departure, with Ray Giles playing as a wing after returning from Cardiff. A 15-9 win over Newbridge brought the quarter-finals and Pontypool were favourites, but Mike Tobin and Ian Spender dominated the lineout and tries came from Phil Ruddall, John Jardine and Neil Forester, plus two Forester penalties in an 18-12 scoreline.

Paul Williams: *"Pontypool arrived brimming with confidence having won 44-7 early in the season, but the squad had undergone major rebuilding and the team that took the field only contained two or three players from that earlier encounter. A key factor was the return of Giles as skipper, who, with an improving pack steered Aberavon to victory.*

Ruddall's try came after Graham Evans produced a classic take-and-give in one movement to send him over. Unfortunately Evans injured his arm and went off. Jardine chased a towering kick which Matthew Silva dropped to claim the second try. Pontypool laid siege, but Aberavon refused to yield, and one could sense Pontypool confidence ebbing away. Forester put it beyond doubt when he crashed through for the final try."

The semi-final against Bridgend at Stradey Park saw the Ravens win 12-6 despite penalties by Lyndon Lewis and Forester. Aberavon lost Tobin and Phil Hamley with injury and a reserve hooker played flanker. Paul Williams: *"The reserve hooker was Anthony Jones from Porthcawl, a big lad and afraid of nobody and subsequently earned himself the nickname 'Billboard' after an incident at Cardiff. He replaced Hamley and blamed himself for conceding a try when he was caught out close to the line. Those nearer the incident said Hamley was felled by a haymaker of a punch."*

Aberavon lost to Notts (6-44) with Wales cap Malcolm Dacey making an appearance and scoring the try. Karl Tapper, a Swedish international No 8, who had played for Aberavon, appeared for The Rest of Europe against Four Home Unions at Twickenham.

Paul Williams: *"New players included Phil Sutton (Neyland); Brian Shenton from Neath Athletic (nicknamed 'Billy' after the comic book character Sporting Billy); Mark 'Twm' Thomas (Neath Ath) and Tony Woodward (Pyle). Brendan Roach was drafted in from Bridgend when Neville Roberts broke a hand and Giles was suspended for being sent off at Glamorgan Wanderers. Graham Evans and his brother Mark also joined."*

In May, Aberavon toured Canada, defeating Frazer Valley President's XV 25-18, then losing 20-35 to Vancouver President's XV and 4-6 to Oak Bay. It ended with a 25-16 win over Canadian champions James Bay, though one newspaper said 16-16! In that final match, skipper Matthews was sent off.

Recalling the tour, Lyndon Lewis and Kevin George agreed it was particularly tough, saying: *"It was as if one team passed it on to another that they had to try and punch us out of games. But, they reckoned without 'Mull' (Colin Roberts) in our pack. We had a drink a day after a match and a man came in the bar with half his face in a mess. We laughed and said the one 'Mull' hit would look like that. Later we found it WAS the man 'Mull' hit!"*

Talking of unusual visages, and bearing once more in mind the justifiable claim of the Aberavon 'borough' to be the actor's cradle of Wales, it was during this season that Sir Anthony Hopkins' most famous role hit the silver screen. Aberavon's players may not have suffered in Silence, but suffer they more than once did as Lambs to the slaughter!

The WRUs Heineken League started in 1990-91. Aberavon were in Division 1, one below the Premier Division. They finished fourth of eight – W8, L6. Ray Giles was captain and in all games it was: W 18, L 25. Andrew Graham from Porthcawl scored 24 tries (12 in the league) with 15 each from Gwilym Wilkins and Dafydd Roberts.

Paul Williams: *"Of the newcomers, Graham was a good wing, who played in all the league games. Carmarthen centre Anthony Dragone came from Maesteg and fly half Matthew McCarthy from Taibach Youth."*

Matthew McCarthy, Hughes Hall and Cambridge University, was the star of a Varsity match.

Matthew was a talented young man who became the star of a Varsity match for Cambridge, totally outplaying Gareth Rees (Newport/Canada) and winning a Wales 'B' cap. He moved to Neath, returned, but was injured and later transferred to Bonymaen. He said: *"I did not quite fulfil my potential."* If not, it was a pretty good attempt.

A schoolteacher, he became backs coach at several clubs and his performance against Newport on a Sunday was televised and produced rave reports, but Aberavon lost 22-36. The first league match was an 18-3 win at Tredegar and the first home game a 13-6 victory over Maesteg, before Graham scored four tries against Penarth.

Paul Williams: *"An amusing story came at Tredegar, when Mike Tobin was injured and substituted. As he came off, he stopped at the snack bar and left munching on a burger to the amusement of spectators. 'Well, you've got to eat, haven't you?', he said."*

In the Cup, Aberavon beat RTB 48-7 with three tries by John Jardine, but fell 13-23 at Swansea. There was a disastrous 13-64 loss at Newbridge and 0-36 at Pontypool but the double was completed over London Welsh with the Easter meeting being their last for 15 years. Mark Thomas was sent off at Newport and Kevin George at home to Bridgend.

Season 1991-92 saw Anthony Woodward as skipper, while Ray Giles went to Kenfig Hill and Matt McCarthy to Neath. Richard Diplock returned, with newcomers including Dean Griffiths, Wayne 'Smiler' Morris, Mark Smith, Kevin Allen, Lee Williams, David 'Dambuster' Edwards from Cwmavon (famous for his 'airplane spins' after scoring) and David Harwood, a South African of Port Talbot ancestry, who unfortunately sustained a serious knee injury.

Brendan Roach was a more permanent addition, but the main signing was David Love from Ystradgynlais, via Ebbw Vale. He scored a club record 349 points with 176 in the league and was the only one to play all 18 league games. On April 11 he passed 300 against Cross Keys and a week later at Penarth he overtook the record held by Mike Lewis.

The final league match, at Glamorgan Wanderers, saw Exeter University student Lyndon Lewis at his best. He scored two tries in the 19-6 victory – one being a brilliant effort that covered 80 metres. Anthony Dragone ran in 26 tries overall (12 in the league) including four against the British Army of the Rhine, and Love landed eight conversions against Ystalyfera.

Aberavon improved to 11th in the 'championship' and 2nd in Division 2 (renamed from Division 1, as the Premier had now become Division 1!). It meant promotion behind South Wales Police after two draws against them, and it was P 18, W 11, D 3, L 4 in the league.

The three clashes with the Police included a league encounter when Mark Smith and the Police's Wales cap Hugh Williams-Jones were dismissed. Hugh received two weeks but Mark had a 10-week ban! Double standards? The Cup was a tragedy, beating Garndiffaith 32-7 before losing to the Police at Waterton Cross 10-19. Kevin Allen won a Wales under-21 cap and though there were numerous losses, scores were not that high, though Bridgend won 52-4.

Lyndon Lewis was captain for 1992-93. It was a mixed season, with disaster in the Cup, but the club stayed in Division 1 (now the top division) by finishing 9th of 12 (P 22, W 7, L 15). Overall they were 12th in the Welsh Championship (W 13, L 18), but the full record including 'friendlies' was: P 40, W 20, L 20. David Love scored 171 points (122 in the league).

The try was now worth five points and there were plenty conceded, the lowest ebb being perhaps between a 0-50 loss at Newport in the league and a Cup defeat by 5-9 at Fleur de Lys, when Richard Diplock scored the only try, but James Egan took 'Flower' through with three penalties – and the Division 3 side deserved it.

Nevertheless, there were wins to savour. South African side Griqualand West were beaten 67-19 with tries by Phil Middleton 2, Anthony Jones 2, two penalty tries, Chris Kinsey, Dylan Davies, Richard Diplock, Phil Hamley and Wayne Morris. Neil Griffiths kicked six conversions.

On Boxing Day Aberavon defeated Neath at home for the first time in eight years and in 18 successive games against them. The win was by 25-14 with a penalty try and tries from scrum half Alan Davies, hooker Ian Evans and flanker Geraint Thomas. Fly half Craig Ryan from Trimsaran, a Wales Youth cap, kicked five points.

Paul Williams: *"The Boxing Day win saw Justin Hughes get the better of Leighton Gerrard at the scrums – something that was instrumental in the penalty try that sealed the win. Neath had won 17 in a row and were after the Aberavon record of 21 (1973-81)."*

Aberavon repeated the win, in league play, by 13-12 with a John Jardine try and eight points from Love and leaders Swansea were halted 12-6. Love placed two penalties and a drop goal and centre Gareth Thomas added a penalty.

Paul Williams: *"The win over Swansea cost them the league title. It should have been more as highlights clearly showed that Kinsey had grounded the ball for a try, but the referee was unsighted. Kinsey, a hardworking flanker from Taibach, was around for quite a long time though he had a season at Bridgend. On a memorable occasion he was pressed into service at lock in Cross Keys, but we still won. There was also Alan Williams, the ex-Swansea and Barbarians scrum half, who was the father of Wales scrum half Rhodri Williams."*

Scaling the heights: Allan Martin.

Andrew Graham returned from Maesteg and new faces had included the popular, wholehearted Kinsey. Wayne Morris played for Wales under-21s against Ireland and Bob Harwood was made a life member.

Allan Martin made his final appearance in December 1992 – a home victory over Pontypridd – but claims of 700 appearances seem very unlikely and it was probably nearer 500, as his 23 years with the club had gaps with Llanelli, Penarth and Wales, as well as injury and tours, plus a spell in South Africa.

Centre John Jardine was captain for 1993-94 but the big problem that players and supporters had seemed to be with team manager Clive Rowlands and coach Ian Bremner. By March they were dismissed, while David Love had gone to Ystradgynlais after one match, Adrian Varney to Neath, Mark Evans to Swansea and others also moved on.

Division 1 had opened with a 3-59 loss at Cardiff and though it was followed by wins over Dunvant and Cross Keys, there followed a draw and eight defeats, one of which, the 20-59 league defeat at Bridgend saw an EGM called. Paul Williams: *"The Aberavon committee were left in no doubt as to the feelings of the membership with an emergency committee meeting called.*

Clive Rowlands, team manager.

The proposal was to sack Rowlands and Bremner and, with only a month remaining, to let four senior players, including Lyndon Lewis, take the reins. It was carried unanimously."

Still, relegation could have been averted with a draw in the final match at home to Pontypridd. Paul Williams: *"The final match was heartbreaking as the goalkicking form of Lyndon Lewis and Gareth Thomas deserted them. Just one kick would have seen Aberavon home, but all they had were near misses and a 5-7 loss. A win for Bridgend at Dunvant would have saved Aberavon and condemned Dunvant to relegation. Dunvant had Richard Llewellyn sent off early on, but Bridgend failed to get the result.*

"Among the new faces were Adrian Bucknall's brother, Andrew, nephews of the former centre Billy Pascoe. Scrum half Jason Thrupp was around for a while and fly half Nick Griffiths was in his second spell. Simon Hutchinson from Resolven and Llanelli under-21s was a great little wing." But there was still relegation, finishing 11th of 12 (P 22, W 6, D 1, L 15), and 13th in the 'Championship' (P 31, W 11, D 1, L 19).

The Cup had brought no joy, either, as despite a win away to Rhiwbina (37-3) on a school pitch in Cardiff, Aberavon fell 0-29 at the next hurdle at Pontypridd. Jardine played in the West Wales team that lost to Japan at Narberth and Wayne Morris played for Wales under-21s. Scrum half Patrick Horgan burst on the scene in the final month and policeman Dafydd Owen was another who impressed.

Darryl Jones, coach.

In 1994-95, Neath's former Oxford University fly half Darryl Jones was coach and took Aberavon to the Division 2 title as they were promoted back to the top flight, skippered by Brian Shenton.

In the league, full back Don Davies from Pyle scored 110 points and Mark Watts from Maesteg 103 with Pat Horgan scoring eight tries. Overall, it was Davies 127 points, Watts 150 and Horgan nine tries.

Five league wins came before losses at Ebbw Vale and home to Bonymaen. Then came 10 victories before a shaky finish. A loss at Abercynon was followed by a win over South Wales Police, then a controversial 30-29 win at Bonymaen with 25 points by Watts plus a Barry Grabham try.

The last two matches were a disaster with a 27-33 home loss to Narberth and a 15-16 defeat at Llanharan as Watts kicked all the points. It was a title win but the signs were that Aberavon would struggle in the following season. There had been a 33-32 win over Llanelli with 18 points from Sean Holley, but losing margins included 40 points at Abertillery, 27 at Abercrave and a 7-33 defeat to a South African Development XV (Emerging Springboks).

Sean Holley, playing career cut short.

Paul Williams: *"Some senior players were unhappy with Darryl's 'schoolteacher' approach and his recruitment policy from Neath Tertiary College, of whom he was in charge. He left and his successor was former Neath centre Glen Ball, who switched from Bonymaen.*

"The 30-29 win at Bonymaen clinched promotion, but was clouded in controversy regarding Mark Watts' late drop-goal in the gathering gloom. Referee Paul Adams signalled it was over. Others were to say differently.

"No 8 Dafydd Owen went to Treorchy, but returned and was an old-fashioned grafting forward. Barry Grabham was a fine wing; Mark Watts a good utility back; fly half Paul Williams was much-travelled and Sean Holley a promising full back, who wrecked his knee against Gary Teichmann's Emerging Springboks), an injury which ended his playing career. Others included Nicky Stubbs (Vardre), James Davies (Pyle) and Stephen Ford, son of former club forward Len Ford."

In the league it was P 22, W 17, L 5 to edge out Ebbw Vale and Abercynon by a single point. In the Championship there was a rise to 5th place (P 33, W 20, L 13). But, there was tragedy in the Cup as after wins over Abercrave (21-6 away), Tenby Utd (6-3 away) and Cardiff Inst (21-15), the 'Wizards' collapsed in the quarter-finals at Cardiff, who won 73-3, including 10 tries in Aberavon's biggest-ever Cup loss.

Pat Horgan and Ford both played for Wales under-21s and Stephen Wharmby was appointed secretary, later replacing Peter Stevens as the 'PA person' after the latter's sad death.

On August 26th 1995 in Paris, Wales' Chair of the IRB, the late Vernon Pugh, QC, declared the game of rugby union 'open' and professional. A brave new world?.... the 1995-96 season proved the worst in Aberavon history. They finished 18th and bottom of

Glen Ball coached Aberavon from August 1995 to 1998.

the 'Championship' for the first time ever. The Western Mail used the W 3, L 19 tally, though of course more than 22 games were played.

However, that said it all about a side that had lost Pat Horgan, Paul Williams and John Funnell to Neath, though coach Glen Ball was now teamed with Jeremy Cooper, the former Llanelli flanker, as forwards coach with Colin Laity, the splendid Cornwall, Cardiff Institute and Neath player, at centre.

In Division 1, Aberavon finished 11th of 12 (P 22, W 3, L 19) – how strange that the Western Mail had decided that no further Cup or friendlies had been played! They were nearly correct regarding Cup rugby, as the 'Wizards' crashed 0-27 at home to Caerphilly. However, there were around 20 other matches played that season!

The points-against league figure included 70 at Pontypridd; 66 at Swansea; 57 at Cardiff and finally 17-95 at Neath, conceding 15 tries. In the final league match, Aberavon scored six tries (three by Nick Stork) and still lost 34-41 at Newbridge.

Paul Williams: *"Of the new faces – props Robert Price and Alun Bevan came from Bonymaen; Richard Jasper was a fine prop; Mark Bernard was a New Zealander who settled in Swansea; lock Steve Pearce a policeman from Old Illtydians; lock Paul Clapham, an Englishman who arrived from Kenfig Hill, while there were back-rowers Howard Merrett (Llanharan) and Andrew Miers (Bonymaen) and also, a young man who made his debut in the opening game at Newport on September 2nd.*

"That debutant was none other than Richard ('George') Morris, a Wales under-21 cap from Neath, who was to become a legend in Aberavon history. "Despite the poor playing record, the players seemed happier with the coaching but the problem was that they took over a successful second-tier squad and had the thankless task of preparing for top-tier rugby. Although a decent recruitment policy brought in several players who would develop distinguished careers at the club, they weren't yet prepared for the step up and confidence quickly eroded as defeats mounted.

"Laity was a class act, playing a lot at fly half and revealing what a naturally talented player he was. Pearce was physically imposing and a terrific ball carrier, but plagued with back problems, while Morris was young and raw, but from day one showed the potential that he was to fulfill as one of the best ball carrying No. 8s in Wales. In the longer term, they began to gel into a promising squad, but the results spoke for themselves."

The 1996-97 season was a total and utter disaster for very many of the leading clubs in Wales. The new Anglo-Welsh Competition (unsponsored) never came near to finishing. What did finish was the now-useless unofficial Welsh 'Championship', which had effectively been a joke for many years.

Aberavon, captained by Colin Laity, won the title in May with their 22nd match of 22. The *Welsh Brewers Annual*, sticking to the original fixture

Richard 'George' Morris was to become Aberavon's record try-scorer.

patterns and ignoring weather and other postponements, said it was won in game 19 – the annual proving incorrect, as usual, in each division. Aberavon were not promoted, as the WRU changed the rules during the season. Club rugby was going downwards fast as the goalposts were changed more often in the WRU committee room than on the pitches of Wales, it seemed.

Alun Bevan and Steve Pearce were sent off and then both classed as blameless by the WRU. In the league, Jason Ball, son of coach Glen, scored 135 points and Richard ('Spud') Lewis and Daran Griffiths (debut on August 31) scored nine tries. Indeed, 28 players scored tries with the highest score being 74-5 against Abercynon and in Division 2 it was: P 22, W 16, D 1, L 5 with 107 tries, finishing with nine wins and a draw in the last 10 games.

It went to the last game on a Friday night at Ystradgynlais, where after 40 minutes the 'Wizards' were struggling. Then came a burst of scoring, with six tries being scored in all. Glen Ball waited for the trophy to be presented. No WRU official was present. Nobody was interested. It was another PR and wider failure in the so-called professional era.

If that was bad, the 'Anglo-Welsh' was a bigger fiasco. Some 12 Welsh and 11 English clubs played in four groups. Only Coventry and Notts finished, though Aberavon were unbeaten with victories over Notts (69-13 away) and Bedford (32-12 home and 19-17 away). They drew at home with Wakefield (27-27) and Notts (13-13), but Wakefield away was not played.

Nick Stork scored three tries at Notts and Richard Diplock was sent off against Wakefield: and that was the end of another 'useless' competition. Paul Matthews and Barry Grabham had gone to Neath, but newcomers included scrum half Andrew Jacobs. In the Cup, Aberavon won 39-22 at Maesteg before losing 8-32 home to Ebbw Vale.

New WRU rules (of course!) were to be tried out from September 1997 – two bonus points could be gained; teams to go off in the interval if they wished; three points for a win; one for a draw; six subs could play and Division 2 was increased to 16 clubs. What next?

Paul Williams: *"The Anglo-Welsh was abandoned. No sponsor, no trophy. Aberavon and Wakefield were unbeaten in their group when interest finally petered out.* (Mark you, the Wizards have since fared better than Wakefield RU club: founded in 1901, they floundered and folded in 2004, a victim of the problems of professional rugby union.)

"Aberavon's games against Bedford stick in the memory. At home Daran Griffiths intercepted a pass from Martin Offiah's fingertips and ran 80 metres to score. At Bedford, the home side featured Canadian captain Norm Hadley at lock, plus an assortment of Pacific Islanders. Their backs included Offiah and Paul Turner, but they conceded their only home defeat that season.

"In the league, Aberavon needed a four-try win at Ystradgynlais to beat Llandovery to the title. There were hundreds of supporters from both clubs and nerves got the better of the 'Wizards' during the first half, passes going astray and even reliable Jason Ball dropping the ball with the line at his mercy. Eventually, they got their act together with the all-important try coming when Rob Price crashed over and the title was secured with a bit to spare.

"On October 5, at home to Ystradgynlais in the league, a second-half replacement was a teenage debutant fly half and Wales Youth cap by the name of Jamie Davies...." Yes, the legend had begun. The boy was to become the highest-ever scorer for Aberavon, the highest in the Premiership for any club and the highest in the whole of league rugby for any club. His debut, though, brought only a penalty and a conversion.

Colin Laity had his second season as captain when Aberavon competed in Division 1 (there was once more a Premier Division!) in 1997-98. A loss at Treorchy was a set-back but then came a run of 11 wins and two draws that included a 23-17 victory away to leaders Caerphilly. With nine games remaining, form dipped alarmingly, so much so that six of the next seven were lost. With two games remaining it seemed Treorchy would be second though Aberavon then beat Pontypool 45-22.

On May 16, Treorchy beat Maesteg 73-24 and Aberavon had to go on a Wednesday to Abertillery in a must-win situation. They did, by 19-5 with Richard Diplock outstanding. The Cup saw a 26-10 win over Bedwas as No 8 Lloyd Griffiths scored three tries and Maesteg were defeated 35-15. It meant a visit to St Helen's, where Swansea thrashed Aberavon 66-12 in a 10-try blitz.

Colin Laity.

Paul Williams: *"Aberavon's new faces included lock Paul Owen, who transferred from Kenfig Hill. Prop Neil Hennessy (later a noted referee) played while studying at Swansea University and was capped for Wales Students and Under-21s. Lloyd Griffiths was No. 8 and Chris Lewis full back/wing, who later returned to Bonymaen and badly broke his leg in a Tovali Cup final."* Jamie Davies, meanwhile, had returned to Aberavon Quins for 12 months.

The league saw W 20, D 2, L 8 with 104 tries, gaining a runners-up spot to Caerphilly, but finishing 19 points behind the Cheesemen. Jason Ball scored 130 points; Andrew Jacobs 11 tries and Richard Lewis 10. Caerphilly were promoted and Newport (deservedly beaten 33-22 by Division Three Rhymney in the Ben Francis Cup Final) were relegated from the Premier Division.

Or were they? Transfers flew around: then in late August 1998, with no worthwhile players left to sign, came the news that since Cardiff and Swansea had withdrawn for their 'rebel' season, Aberavon were promoted and Newport stayed up.

So, despite captain Justin Hughes giving excellent service as hooker and prop, Aberavon in 1998-99 were again lambs to the slaughter: and they WERE slaughtered. Worse still was another crazy WRU decision to take the bottom-half of the table and let them all play each other again! Caerphilly actually beat Newport five times – four league and one Cup.

Paul Williams: *"Aberavon moved up to the Premier Division at a few days' notice with a squad assembled to play at a lower level. A predictably disastrous season was then used by the WRU as a stick with which to beat the club during disputes that arose in subsequent seasons over repeated changes to promotion rules."*

Rob Cole was on the ball in *The Independent*: '*The fact that two clubs were given less than a week to prepare for life in the top flight has made it difficult for them to gear up for the new campaign. The money they were expecting from the WRU as First Division sides was around £70,000, while in the Premiership it will be closer to £400,000. So when the matches kick-off today, with Newport hosting Neath and Aberavon travelling to Bridgend, the two replacements will be at an immediate disadvantage, having budgeted for the lower division.*

It means there is likely to be an "us and them" scenario.... the have-nots will be Newport and Aberavon, Bridgend and Neath, the Welsh All Blacks folding during the summer with debts of £600,000, only to be saved by the WRU. If it is not quite a recipe for great competition, at least the rule changes have given some new impetus to the tournament.

As well as playing each other on a home and away basis, the top four sides will then play each other twice more in the race for the title, while the bottom four will battle it out to avoid relegation. Add in four matches against overseas opposition in the Challenge Trophy, and a potential five ties in the Swalec Cup, and the fixture list, at least, is more extensive. But never mind about the width, what about the quality? Exactly!

There were many embarassing days including 28-64 at Pontypridd (Rhys Shorney 7 tries); 24-63 at Neath; 10-83 at Llanelli (13 tries); 26-68 at home to Bridgend; 10-87 at Castres and 13-97 at Montauban on a Wednesday night, when Aberavon assembled a host of loan players from lower division clubs who never appeared again. Gerald Davies in *The Times* asked how could a part-time side go to France in midweek and play against full-time

Rugby League star Gary Schofield.

professionals? Those in higher places did not appear to even care.

One answer was to sign Gary Schofield, the 46-times-capped Rugby League centre, but he was 36 – and though certainly not a 'never-was', was then nearer a 'has-been'. His debut was away to Spain at El Ferrol. Yes, Aberavon won 18-6, but after five more games, Schofield went back to the North of England.

The coaching team comprised two men who had not previously met and neither had played for Aberavon. Fly half Steve Brown and the rugged Newport No 8 Roger Powell had a thankless task and were on a hiding to nothing. On the lighter side, at the Brewery Field, Bridgend's international lock Chris Stephens parked his new sponsored BMW behind the posts and Crispin Cormack's kick smashed the windscreen!

The Cup saw wins over Carmarthen Quins (49-22) and Ystrad Rhondda (37-7 away) before a narrow and needless 12-20 loss at home to Cardiff. It was 12-13 until the last minute when Rees should have dropped a winning goal, but instead his pass was intercepted by Gareth Thomas, who strolled away to clinch it.

Then came another weird competition – the WRU Challenge Trophy. Four games were played – all home – beating Georgia 42-0 and Natal Wildebeests 20-14, but losing to Canada 0-10 and Edinburgh Reivers by 14-39.

In the Premier Division Aberavon were: P 20, W 2, L 18 and in the new 'insane' European Shield it was: W 1, L 5. The complete record in all games was: W 8, L 26, as Cerith Rees from Llandovery scored 156 league points, including 11 tries.

Other new faces included Shane McIntosh (Dale's brother), Damian Neill, Paul Jones, Ed Lewsey, Peter Roberts, Tim Green, Aaron Hamilton (from Hawke's Bay) and prop Lloyd Howell, who made his debut at Pontypridd on September 12.

Meanwhile, down in Division 3 West, Jamie Davies scored 17 tries in 230 league points for Aberavon Quins, aided by ex-Aberavon captain Gary Matthews, but in March, the 33-yr-old former Taibach, Aberavon and Bridgend forward Nigel Spender tragically died while jogging in Port Talbot. He was a building surveyor for Neath and Port Talbot Council and a crew member of the Port Talbot lifeboat, having retired from rugby with a neck injury 18 months earlier.

More happily, a dinner at the Afan Lido had over 700 guests to honour the First Lady of Aberavon and Welsh rugby – the remarkable Mrs. Evelyn Mainwaring. Comedian Colin Price summed it up by saying: *"only two other Welsh personalities could have filled the hall – Shirley Bassey and Tom Jones."* Fitting, really: she could certainly claim 'I am what I am', and has surely been the most famous regular attender at the 'Green, green grass' of her home turf at the Talbot.

Mrs. Evelyn Mainwaring in full flow to a young Non Evans

10

1999-2009

Canny O'Cally takes over and titles are gained.....

It was all change in 1999-2000 as Chris O'Callaghan took over as coach in November after Steve Brown and Roger Powell were dismissed. Aberavon had lost nine of their 13 league matches and thereafter won nine of the remaining 17, notching 104 points in successive outings against Abertillery (46-17 away) and UWIC (58-21 home). Milennium magic? – or some canny recruitment, man-management and hard work, maybe.

O'Callaghan brought in New Zealander Scott Leighton and he shared the kicking with Matt McCarthy, who was back with the club. Matt scored 137 league points while Scott scored 127. Richard Morris ran in 13 league tries and despite finishing 8th in Division 1, the Wizards were second-highest try-scorers with 101 with lock Mark Evans now the club captain.

O'Callaghan's reign began at Abercynon, where Aberavon led 3-2 on tries, but lost 20-21. He lost Daran Griffiths for a short spell at Swansea; Cerith Rees and Andrew Jacobs to Neath; Barry Grabham to Pyle; Lyndon Lewis to Vardre; Peter Roberts and Richard Lewis to Bonymaen; Justin Hughes to Caerphilly and both Stephen Ford and Richard Jasper to Bridgend.

New faces included Barry Maddocks (Dunvant), Ian Moore (Cwmavon/ Neath), Ian Jones (Llanelli), Sam Greenaway (Treorchy/Penarth), Paul Bamsey (Taibach), Andrew James (Seven Sisters), Gareth King, Jason Hyatt (Llanelli), Colin Noon, Ian Strang, Mervyn Meredith and Dan McShane.

In the Cup Aberavon led Wrexham 49-7 in pouring rain before it was abandoned with the result standing; Resolven were beaten 46-9, but then came a loss by 6-17 at Neath. Jamie Davies rattled up 235 points with Aberavon Quins in Division 3 West, including 12 tries and O'Callaghan's eyes were on him. Paul Williams: *"Leighton came as a fly half, but played his best rugby at inside-centre, where he was a guiding hand and mentor to the young Jamie Davies. Scott's contribution to Aberavon between 2000 and 2003 is well remembered.*

If Andrew John had not agreed to take the helm as managing director by 2000, Aberavon may have long since gone the way of Tredegar. We are thankful that

Andrew successfully changed the culture at the club into a professionally run organisation with just three directors. A new constitution was drafted by the membership at an EGM and Andrew took the reins. Chris O'Callaghan halted, and then reversed the club's slide."

O'Callaghan commented: " I sent Eddie Jones to watch Jamie Davies play, relying implicitly on his judgement of players: he summed up Jamie as someone who 'kicked the ball further than most people go on holidays but was quieter than the salad bar in Butlins!'

Chris O'Callaghan.

"The captain was again Mark Evans, brother of Graham and British amateur heavyweight champion Kevin, both 'Wizards' themselves. Leighton and Natano Tiatia came from British Steel where they were with another Kiwi, Tristan Meo: all from Wellington and all excellent. Scott and 'Tano' became regulars and both were immense in turning Aberavon's fortunes around." The League tallies were: P 30, W 13, D 0. L 17.

In 2000-01 Aberavon were to win Division 1. Paul Williams was able to conclude: "A new era had begun – no more committee, but a board of directors in Andrew John (Managing Director), Steve Wharmby (Secretary), Mike Read (Director of Finance) and O'Callaghan."

Jamie Davies had rejoined the club and kicked all 15 points in the draw against Carmarthen, scoring 223 in the league and 325 in all. Wing Lee Abdul (Rumney) ran in 17 of the 114 league tries with Sam Greenaway on 14 and Richard Morris 10. Hat-tricks went to Greenaway (twice); Paul Bamsey and Daran Griffiths, while Abdul scored four at Llanharan.

Other newcomers included Ricky Price (SW Police), Dan Hawkins (Bonymaen), Mike Harris, Steve Rees (Neath/SW Police), Andrew Thomas and Greg Dix (Wales Districts cap from Tondu/Maesteg). Skipper Mark Evans was injured and Hawkins mostly led, while O'Callaghan had taken less than 12 months to get a winning combination.

The side finished 12 points clear of Dunvant with P 30, W 26, D 1, L 3, the draw coming in the opener at home to Carmarthen Quins. They were unbeaten at home and finished with eleven successive league wins. The Cup brought wins over Merthyr (34-0) and Cross Keys (31-8), but Newport were too strong at Rodney Parade and eight tries were conceded in losing 18-56. On January 31, Jamie Davies scored 33 points (3t, 6c, 2p) in a home friendly against British Steel (63-0).

The Welsh-Scottish ('Premier' Division) was to be ring-fenced (didn't stop the Scots leaving after three years!) so there was no promotion for Aberavon when Cross Keys came down to reduce the numbers: 11 in the top division, 17 in Division One!

There was an astonishing race for the Division 1 title in 2001-02 between Aberavon and Pontypool. Newcomers at the Talbot included Marvin Thomas (Pencoed School), Alastair Rogers (a Margam boy who by 2017 was part of the NZ backroom team that had won two World Cups), Owen Rutley (Cowbridge) and Matthew Back, capped by Wales in 1995.

Steve Rees took the captaincy and the season began with a 10-20 loss at Pontypool. Three more defeats followed, then Greenaway scored a hat-trick against Llanharan in a super run of 20 successive wins including 10-9 home revenge over Pontypool. Jamie scored 24 points against Glamorgan Wanderers and 21 against Bedwas; Treorchy fell 57-0, Llanharan 88-7, with 14 tries including four by Greenaway and 28 points by Davies.

There was a shock with a 5-14 loss at Whitland, but the 'Wizards' defeated Bonymaen 26-12 and Merthyr 65-10 at The Wern as Greenaway scored three of the 12 tries. The penultimate game at Tondu was a 63-21 win with 10 tries, including a hat-trick by Jamie.

The final match saw 14 tries needed to overtake Pontypool, who had scored 27 in their last two games. Aberavon did it, however, with a 72-24 win over Dunvant at Broadacre. Paul Williams: *"It took Aberavon a while to get going and Dunvant scrapped for half an hour, but a Dan Hawkins try late in the first half broke their resolve and the flood gates opened. Scott Leighton scored the 14th try on 78 minutes. Referee Clayton Thomas had said he had nine minutes left, but after Scott's try said he'd call a halt if both captains agreed: and they did."*

Both the 'Wizards' and Pooler had: P 32, W 27, D 0, L 5 in their League clashes, with 81 points apiece. The clubs scored 152 tries each, but Aberavon had the better points-difference. Jamie Davies scored 370 league points (16t, 69c, 48p) and set a new club record of 461 overall (17t, 92c, 64p). Scott Leighton notched 128 league points and league tries came from Sam Greenaway (25), Daran Griffiths (17) and Ricky Price (10). During the season, Michael Hook had gone to Newport and gained Wales under-21 caps to add to his under-19 honours.

That year the WRU had gone as far as allowing a play-off against the bottom Premier club to 'earn' promotion. That was Caerphilly. The Cheesemen came to Aberavon and won 17-13, then five days later at Virginia Park, triumphed again, 49-14 (66-27 on aggregate). There had been successive Division 1 titles, yet no promotion! Efforts in the courtroom and an EGM of the WRU to overturn that situation were doomed to failure. The WRU might have regularly held their AGMs (and frequent EGMs!) at the local Princess Royal Theatre, but that was as close as they and the club often got.

In a friendly, Aberavon defeated the 7th Parachute Regiment of the Royal Horse Artillery by a club record 102-0 with 16 tries and Jamie scoring 22 points, and the Cup saw the only clash to date between the clubs of the authors: hosts Aberavon beat Rhymney 52-20, with 27 points from Leighton. Whitland were downed 27-9 away, but 'Avon lost 16-24 at home to Cardiff. The 'Wizards' trailed but Leighton kicked two penalties and a drop so Cardiff led 21-16 with five minutes remaining. Then, replacement Iestyn Harris landed a clinching penalty.

Bonymaen captain and lock Chris Gittins had signed for Aberavon in September 2001. He became club captain for the 2002-03 season and much

Scrum half Daniel Hawkins, who was later joined by brother David.

of the three that followed. He began his term with another battle between Aberavon and Pontypool for the title. This time Pooler won, but surprise, surprise, the WRU pulled the plug on promotion once again.

Newcomers included Kristian Owen and Chris Perry from Merthyr, while Lloyd Howell and Mervyn Meredith returned. A club record was set with a win at Chepstow in a friendly by 108-0. Morris, Paul Bamsey and David Hawkins (on debut) scored hat-tricks and there were 18 tries in total.

Early results included losses away to Pontypool and Cross Keys, then 14 successive victories in all games; a loss at Carmarthen in the Cup; another 11 wins and then a disastrous 12-40 home loss to Pontypool, before the season ended with a win at Blackwood. The 161 league tries will no doubt last forever as a club record. Pontypool borrowed a local pigeon fancier's trophy as again, the WRU did not bother to turn up! The Pooler defeat was the Wizards' first at home in the league after 29 successive victories.

Again the two clubs tied on points (90), wins (30) and defeats (4), but Pontypool won 194-161 on tries this time. Jamie Davies set a magnificent club record of 515 points (14t, 107c, 72p, 5dg) but of course didn't talk about it much, and a league record 451 (10t, 85c, 72p, 5dg). Also in the league, Richard Morris set a forwards' record with 19 tries, while Lee Abdul scored 21 (27 in all matches), Owen and Ricky Price both gained 13 and

Skipper and lock Chris Gittins in his Barbarian jersey.

there were 10 each from Sam Greenaway and David Hawkins (Danny's brother).

Hat-tricks came from Abdul (twice), Owen, Morris, Tommy Price and flanker Andrew Thomas.

In the Cup, Aberavon fell at Carmarthen Quins (12-13) after having defeated Abertillery 93-0 with 15 tries, including four by Abdul and nine conversions from Jamie Davies. Shortly afterwards the Gwent club folded temporarily, having to start again at the bottom of the League, then Division Five: a salutary warning as to what might have also happened to a number of the 'Merit Table' clubs in the aftermath of 'official' professionalism.

Pontiac Signs and a local art teacher, Malcolm Hockin (father of lock Danny) contributed a mural of a fierce-looking Wizard to the wall of the visitors' dressing-room with the words: 'Welcome to the World of Hurt.' It was another effort by the canny O'Callaghan to strike fear into teams who came to the Talbot Athletic Ground, and apart from the Pooler reverse, seemed to have a point.

In season 2003-04 the Ospreys were born as one of the five (at first) regions or super-clubs designed to save Welsh rugby. At Aberavon, theoretically under the Ospreys' wing, Chris Gittins was again captain, but Paul Bamsey had gone to Neath, Barry Maddocks to Carmarthen Quins/Llanelli and Lee Abdul to Cardiff Blues. Lennie Woodard (Pontypool) scored seven tries then moved to Ebbw Vale; Jamie Summers came and returned to Treorchy; Chris Perry went to Llanharan and Kristian Owen to Ebbw Vale.

New faces included Wales cap Darryl Williams (Llanelli/Bonymaen) and flanker Dean Thomas (Swansea), who soon left. Paul Breeze (Cwmavon), Darren Ryan (Cardiff), Rhyddian Gierat (Glyncorrwg), Matthew Bradley and Craig Moses also started.

With regional rugby now above the WRU's Leagues, the domestic Premier Division had been increased to 16 and, at last, Aberavon had been promoted into it. In that league, Richard Morris and Ricky Price scored nine tries apiece, while in the Cup, Aberavon reached the semi-final and scored 173 points in five ties. They beat Merthyr 43-13, Banwen 45-15, Bonymaen 25-16, then 38-21 at Cross Keys in a quarter-final with 23 points from Jamie: but in a semi-final at the Millennium Stadium, they lost 22-33 to Caerphilly, both sides scoring three tries.

Morris and Daran Griffiths both passed 100 career tries, while there were losses to Neath by 18-43 and 21-33, but doubles over Llanelli and Cardiff. There was also a 102-5 league win over Caerphilly, Jamie Davies scoring 32 points, and among the 16 tries were those by the splendid Mike Harris and hooker Jason Hyatt, who retired after 140 appearances. Jamie scored 28 points in a win over Carmarthen Quins.

It was the best season for O'Callaghan, then, and Aberavon had played splendidly to reach fourth spot: P 30, W 17, L 13, scoring 93 tries. Jamie Davies scored 325 league points and an overall 432 (13t, 77c, 70p, 1dg). He was then just 83 points away from taking Mike Lewis' club record.

In August, Aberavon won 114-0 at Glyncorrwg with Daran Griffiths scoring five of the 18 tries and Richard 'Spud' Lewis 22 points. James Hook made his sole appearance for the club in a friendly against Maesteg.

The season 2004-05 marked the departure of Chris O'Callaghan. Howard Evans stated: *"Chris left and in came former internationals Kevin Hopkins and Mark Jones as back and forward coaches respectively. It was the same day as Sir Clive Woodward announced his England departure. Oddly, Chris had been captain and Clive his vice at Loughborough College.*

"O'Cally 'put backsides on seats' and had said he was stiffening his defence with 'Herbal Viagra'. He never suffered fools gladly and was not popular with the WRU, but stopped the club's decline and put great fear into teams who came to the ground."

Andrew John said: *"We parted by mutual agreement and on the best of terms. What he and team manager Eddie Jones have done for this club has been magnificent."* O'Callaghan added: *"My decision was taken in the best interests of the club. Next week I will be buying a season ticket. I hope the club's record in recent years says it for me. Kevin needs no advice from me while Mark is cutting his teeth, but is a winner and has a brilliant presence in the changing room and on the field."*

Kevin Hopkins admitted his surprise but remarked: *"Chris was the best thing ever for Aberavon. He is a passionate Aberavon man through and through and always very committed. Mark and I now just want to continue all the good work he has done."* So an era ended: with two titles, a runners-up spot and a cup semi-final, while the final season had seen fourth position gained, above Cardiff, Swansea and Llanelli.

There was a surprising start as August's opening friendly against Rotherham was called off because they had – for the moment – gone bust Chris was in charge for four friendlies, all won. The new faces included Chris Wells (Swansea), recovering from a serious knee injury; prop James Jones; Steve Phillips (Neath); versatile Liam Gadd (Maesteg); Adrian Williams and, during the season, wing Richard Carter (Neath), who proved outstanding.

Coach Kevin Hopkins was a Wales cap at centre.

Paul Bamsey returned from Neath and Barry Maddocks was back, but Steve Rees retired after three league games; Chris Gittins went to Neath; Andrew Clatworthy to Swansea; Dan McShane to Cardiff; Greg Dix was loaned to Corus; centre Paul Morgan to Maesteg (another Paul Morgan joined as lock) and Rhyddian Gierat to Bonymaen.

There emerged a splendid young lock Andrew Fisher (Dunvant) and the all-action crowd-pleasing flanker Darryl Thomas (Cwmavon). The downside was the dreadful appearances made by regional players being farmed out – or forced on – the club for various games, not always conducive to harmony within a squad, nor to results. Right at the end of the season came the debut of Paul Breeze's younger brother, Marc, as a flanker.

It was a good start for the coaches as Gadd and Ryan teamed at centre, playing 30 and 26 games respectively; Mike Harris played 28 and he, Wells, Paul Breeze and Lloyd Howell gave Aberavon a formidable scrummage while Ian Moore blossomed into a strong lock and Carter played in 22 of 25 games after joining. However, injuries came to Jamie Davies and, for much of the season, to Danny Hawkins.

The club's best day was a 19-13 Cup win over Neath which included tries by Maddocks and Bamsey. It was the first-ever by Aberavon over Neath in the Cup and the first overall since 1993, but Neath were runaway league champions and their revenge included a 12-try 80-0 stuffing of the 'Wizards' at the Gnoll on Easter Monday in which 'Avon's Michael Hook, back after injury, opposed his brother James.

Aberavon smashed Newbridge 82-3 with Jamie scoring 27 points and Carter grabbing three of the 12 tries. There was a 32-23 win over Cardiff, skipper Dafydd Owen and Carter sharing four tries. Gadd scored a hat-trick against Bedwas and in the Cup, there were wins over Narberth (14-6 away), Vardre (53-0 away), Neath and Newport (18-17) before a 13-33 semi-final loss to Pontypridd at Bridgend with a red card to Darren Ryan.

Nevertheless, fifth spot in the Premier Division was gained: P 32, W 19, D 0, L 13. Jamie scored 217 league points and 272 overall to set a new club record points aggregate, overtaking Mike Lewis' mark. Another former high-scoring fly half, David Love, turned up to congratulate him, though they had never previously met.

Centre pair Liam Gadd and Darren Ryan 'then & now'!

Liam Gadd scored 149 points in all games, including 129 (with 14 tries) in the league, while Carter ran in 16. Richard Morris and Daran Griffiths were both nearing the club record of 125 tries in a career set by Johnny Ring and captain Dafydd Owen retired after the final league match of the season at home to Newport, going out with a try and a 34-21 victory.

In season 2005-06 lock Chris Gittins returned from Neath to once again be skipper. The players and supporters were delighted, while genuinely 'new' faces included Jonathan Thomas (Mumbles, tragically killed in 2015); Gareth

Quite pleased at beating Neath in the Cup at last!

Knox (Swansea); Richard Morgan (Tonmawr); Christian Richards (Dunvant); teenage prop Neil White (Bonymaen); Anthony Edwards (Tonmawr); Ceri Jones (Corus) and Simon Peters (Llangennech). During the season John Leyshon (Neath/Llanharan) also joined.

Mike Harris played in all 30 league matches, Jamie Davies in 29. A sad moment was the death of life member Bob Harwood, who had served 25 years with the club, but coaches Hopkins and Jones had a wonderful start, winning 10 of the first 11 league games (losing by 13-25 at Pontypridd). Jamie kicked 29 points in a 39-7 win over Newport and reached 100 from the first six matches.

Marc Breeze, the former under-16 Wales captain and then under-18 cap, had added the under-21s and scored an unforgetable try in the 42-20 home win over Cardiff, running from halfway with hand held high, and Jamie scored 25 points against Maesteg.

In league games Jamie scored 375 points and overall 429 (11t, 61c, 84p), while he passed 2,500 points in his career at Aberavon. Richard Carter scored 10 league tries. However, the 'Wizards' lost twice to Neath, and prised only two wins from the last nine games: but finished a creditable fourth in the Premier Division: P 30, W 19, D 0, L 11.

In the Cup Aberavon's 68-15 win over Fleur de Lys contained 28 points by Jamie, followed by a 33-31 win at Ebbw Vale, but then, acting captain Chris Wells was wrongly sent off in a disgraceful decision by the referee as the 'Wizards' lost 7-15 home to Newport. Wells was found to have 'no case to answer', but that was too late. A friendly on a lovely sunny day at Camberley saw London Welsh win 11-6 in the first meeting of the clubs for 14 years. Anthony Edwards, Gareth Knox and Mark Jones all played for a WRU President's XV at Neath.

Mike 'Footy' Harris, a superb prop and clubman.

After eight games of the 2006-07 season (including five league), six had been won, but then coach Kevin Hopkins departed to the Ospreys. Forwards coach Mark Jones was dismissed by the end of December and in came ex-Wales hooker Garin Jenkins, aided by the likeable Jeff Pick. Chris Gittins was again the captain. The team appeared to lose form, though, and Garin departed, with the club advertising in March for a Head Coach for the following season.

Newcomers were James Pike (Glynneath), Ricky Richards (Carmarthen Quins), Richard Thomas (Llangennech) and Robbie Morgan (Corus), while Adrian Williams moved to Carmarthen Quins and Jim Owen retired with injury.

The first league game brought a 19-16 win at Newport and revenge for Richard Morris, whose debut was in a loss at Rodney Parade in 1995. It was Aberavon's first win at Newport since December 11, 1984, in which time they had lost 13 and drawn twice. Jamie Davies was injured and missed the home game with Cardiff, but in stepped teenager James Garland of Vardre for a debut where he kicked six out of six in a 30-21 win.

Neath completed the double, though; Dan Hawkins made his 200th appearance and Steve 'Stella' Davies made his debut from Llangennech with scrum half Chris Morgans also breaking through. A 9-35 home loss to Glamorgan Wanderers saw the 'Wizards' hit the depths; Rob Lewis played three games but left and the season finished with Richard Hibbard (as a replacement flanker) getting a try against Maesteg and Richard Carter scoring four and Steve Davies two in a 45-13 win against Llandovery.

Darren Ryan played in all 26 games, Dan Hawkins, Mike Harris and Chris Gittins in 25, Jamie Davies 24 and Liam Gadd 23. Jamie scored 247 league points and 288 overall with Carter scoring 10 league tries. Aberavon

Ashley Beck, later capped by Wales.

finished seventh of the now 14-stong Premier (do keep up!) with: P 26, W 12, D 2, L 12 and Richard Morris played for the Barbarians against the Combined Services on November 14, scoring a brace of tries.

In the Cup, the 'Wizards' won away at Cwmllynfell (39-14) and Cross Keys (27-15), but Matthew Jones kicked them out by 20-19 at home with the winning Bridgend penalty, despite not being a registered player.

There were new coaches and a new captain for 2007-08 with Simon King, who had played for Aberavon whilst a student, becoming head coach after success at Pontypridd and Nicky Lloyd a fine choice as backs coach, while the magnificent Ian ('Buddah') Moore was the skipper. King and Lloyd also coached Wales under-18s, introducing some fine young players to Aberavon.

All-action flanker and former under-21 cap Chris Davies (Neath), Ricky Thomas and John Phillips (both Porthcawl) and Marc Bennett (Bridgend Athletic) were newcomers, while later Rory Gallagher (Dunvant) and talented under-18 caps Ashley Beck and Justin Tipuric came in. The Hawkins brothers moved to Carmarthen Quins; Chris Kinsey, Ceri Jones and Robbie Morgan to Corus; Richard Thomas to the Blues (then Cardiff and Llanelli); Christian Richards to Dunvant and James Pike to Cwmllynfell.

Dafydd Owen and Dan Hawkins made farewell appearances in the Richard Morris Testimonial match against Neath; centre Darren Ryan moved back to Cardiff after a red card against Ebbw Vale; Daran Griffiths retired with 128 tries and Richard Morris raced on to 132.

Among the league highlights was the debut of Beck, as a replacement,

Justin Tipuric, later capped for Wales and the Lions.

in a 23-12 win over Pontypridd. Cardiff were beaten 42-14 and again used 'passive scrums' and there was a welcome 29-22 Easter Monday win over Neath with Darryl Thomas outstanding. Then came Bedwas and Jamie (on 99 club tries) was tragically injured seconds after unselfishly putting John Leyshon over.

There was no doubting the intent of King and Lloyd, who were not there to be losers. Their first season's League return was: P 26, W 15, D 1, L 10 as the club finished 6th, with Jamie Davies scoring 197 points (245 overall) and Richard Carter 11 tries.

Ian Moore passing, watched by Dan Hawkins.

In friendlies, Greg Dix played a 100th and final game and Dinas Powys were beaten 110-0 as Pike scored four of the 18 tries and James Garland goaled nine. In the Cup the coldest-ever day at Tredegar brought a 29-24 win with Mike Harris suffering a broken thumb. After a 22-7 win over Llandovery, there was 30-23 success against Cardiff, Steve Davies scoring two of the four tries and Ebbw Vale fell 32-22 to a Carter brace, but the 'Wizards' lost 10-33 to Pontypridd in the semi-final at Cardiff, having lost Jamie to a broken arm 14 days earlier.

Ian Moore was again captain for 2008-09 and there was an outstanding Aberavon performance in finishing third in the Premier Division, behind Cardiff and Newport. It was a splendid effort by King, Lloyd and the squad, who beat Cardiff at home 41-40 and Newport away 17-12, yet lost both games to Neath.

Morris played his 400th game and on November 4, Chris Gittins appeared for the Barbarians against the Combined Services (who included his brother at centre). Liam Gadd left for Llanelli, but returned. Richard Hibbard had one game and Ospreys lock Lyndon Bateman did well until injury at Pontypool halted his career. When the 'Wizards' lost home to Neath by 15-17 on Boxing Day, it came after 18 successive home wins in Cup and League.

New faces were wing Chris Lewis; Wales under-18 centre Ben John; scrum half Gavin Hooper; Wales under-18 forward James King; prop Ian Poley; a tremendously strong scrum half David Pritchard (Bridgend Ath); centre Will Price (Tonmawr); centre Luke Hathaway (Bridgend Ath); hooker Brett Thomas and lock Nathan White.

There were even five games as a replacement by the evergreen Brendan Roach from Kenfig Hill and Matthew Jarvis joined from Neath as James Garland departed, disappointed at being dropped after his drop goal winner at Ebbw Vale. Andrew Fisher suffered a career-ending injury after a late tackle at Glamorgan Wanderers. In 26 league games Carter played 25 with Pritchard, Moore and Daryll Thomas on 24.

Richard Thomas returned and scored 15 league tries and Richard Carter 10, while Jamie Davies, despite breaking his arm again, scored 171 points in the league and 232 overall. Richard Morris ended the season having increased the club try-record to 139. The final League record was: P 26, W 17, D 0, L 9 to end six points clear of Llanelli – all three other clubs in the top four having far bigger budgets than Aberavon.

The side visited Cambridge University, losing 10-27 with several youngsters including Matthew Morgan (later a Wales cap), who also scored a try in an 'A' team victory by 24-11 at Cwmavon. Cup wins came over Kidwelly (49-16); Corus (58-19 away, with four tries by Carter); Llantwit Fardre (74-0 with 11 tries) and Newport (20-10), but ended with a 23-26 semi-final defeat by Llanelli at Swansea's Liberty Stadium. Carter scored three tries in the semi-final and took his cup tally to nine for the season.

11

2009-2017

A Happy Ship: a good spell for 'the Wizards'.....

2009-10 saw Ian Moore's third successive season as captain with Aberavon under the continued coaching of Simon King and Nicky Lloyd. Richard Carter went to Carmarthen Quins; James Garland to Swansea; James Jones to Llandovery and Chris Wells retired. Newcomers included Jamie Murphy, Danny Davies, Gavin Ronan from Maesteg and Ben Thomas from Tondu with Christian Richards returning plus a brief interlude from kick-boxing star Rory Saunders on the wing.

In the league, Chris Morgans was to score 10 tries, including three in a 60-27 battering of Pontypool and Matthew Jarvis scored 26 points at Swansea. Draws were for once plentiful: 36-36 at Swansea; 32-32 home to Llandovery; 28-28 at Pontypridd and 31-31 at Cardiff. Last came a 37-36 win at Bedwas where Rhys Webb, later a Wales scrum half, scored two tries, but there were losses at Neath (33-36) and Llandovery (34-52). Jamie Davies scored his 100th league try (35 at Aberavon Quins, 65 Aberavon) at Pontypool.

Lloyd Howell played in 23 league matches with the great clubman Paul Bamsey in 20, plus the play-off. Sam Williams came in late in the season and Academy prop Ryan Bevington, later a Wales cap, scored a superb try against Cardiff.

The Wizards finished a creditable 5th in the Premiership: P 36, W 14, D 4, L 8, scoring 82 tries. Jamie Davies scored 176 league points and 213 overall, while Matthew Jarvis scored 104 in the league and 137 overall, with Aberavon losing a play-off match to Llandovery by 18-35 despite two tries from Ashley Beck.

In the Cup, Aberavon won 40-0 at Beddau and 33-21 home to Cross Keys before losing 16-41 at Pontypridd despite David Pritchard scoring a try after 16 seconds, while Marc Breeze was red-carded by a dreadful decision. The GB/Irish Cup brought wins (19-16 at Llanelli and 10-0 home to Moseley) and losses (home to London Welsh (7-36); away at Bedford (15-17) and away to Ulster A (0-62). A youngster called Tipuric gave an outstanding display of tackling against Moseley....

At the end of the season Chris Morgans moved to Neath; Rory Gallagher to semi-retirement; Paul Breeze retired with neck injuries after 166 appearances and Marc Bennett also left. In September 2009, sadly, the death was announced of one of the oldest Aberavon players – Randall Lewis.

Chris Davies was captain for 2010-11 and newcomers included former Pontypridd skipper Nathan Strong at No. 8, scrum half Andrew Jenkins and Wales under-18 prop Rowan Jenkins, while Will Price and Richard Carter both returned, but Ben Thomas transferred to Bridgend. Ricky Guest went to Carmarthen Quins

Andrew John with Justin Tipuric, Aberavon, Ospreys, Wales & the Lions.

and Luke Hathaway to Swansea, Marc Breeze to London Welsh, via the Ospreys, but he too soon returned. Both Ashley Beck (63 matches, 25 tries) and Justin Tipuric (33) went to the Ospreys and were later capped: 'Tips' is a Lion, too.

At the end of the season, Ian Poley retired; Andrew Jenkins went to Whitland and Matthew Jarvis (52 matches, 556 points) transferred to Connacht. The biggest loss was prop Mike ('Footy') Harris, wrongly forced into retirement after 301 appearances. In the league, Jarvis played 25 matches; Ricky Thomas 23; Andrew Jenkins and Ian Moore both 22. The club finished fourth in the League: P 36, W 17, D 0, L 9, scoring 90 tries.

Jarvis topped all the league scorers with 315 points, including 29 in a 59-15 win over Llanelli and 26 in a 46-40 win over Carmarthen Quins. Carter scored 22 tries, including 17 in the league, the latter being the highest by anyone in the Premiership. He and Beck scored hat-tricks in an 11-try, 75-19 win away to Glamorgan Wanderers. Carter's four tries failed to prevent a 44-46 loss at Swansea, though, followed by a 41-42 loss at Newport four days later.

In the Cup, Aberavon reached the final for the third time, but lost to Pontypridd 24-35 at the Millennium Stadium but only after a late try was ruled out by a touch-judge error. Carter, Strong and Sam Williams scored tries and Jarvis kicked nine points. In the semi-final, a WRU error allowed Llandovery to play Wales cap Dan Evans, but tries from Chris Lewis and Strong beat the 'Drovers' 18-12 on Carmarthen Park. In earlier rounds the 'Wizards' defeated Bedlinog 74-6, Waunarlwydd 33-19 away and Cardiff 19-17 away.

The Cup final side was: Matthew Jarvis; Richard Carter, Will Price, Ashley Beck (Liam Gadd), Ricky Thomas; Jamie Davies, Dan Davies (David Pritchard); Neil White (Lloyd Howell), Marc Breeze, Tony Edwards (James Jones), Ian Moore (Aaron Bray), Sam Williams, James King (Richard Morris), Nathan Strong, Chris Davies (capt.) (Darryl Thomas). Replacements Gadd and Pritchard changed the game and it was the last for the popular Beck.

To that date, Richard Morris had made 478 appearances, Jamie Davies 351, Howell 289, Chris Gittins 254, Moore 231 and Bamsey 228. Sadly, Gittins retired while Jamie scored only 95 points overall. Aberavon beat Cardiff three times, but lost three to Pontypridd. Morris had reached 100 League tries and 148 in all matches; Carter scored 108, Gadd 50 and Richard Thomas 44. Carter, Breeze and Jamie Davies all played for the Barbarians at Richmond, to some effect: Carter (2) and Breeze (with a great run) scored tries and Jamie converted four.

2011-12 found Chris Davies again captain with successful coaches King and Lloyd guiding the ship: the sort of much-needed consistency that had been lacking in some earlier decades. Craig Evans joined from Llangennech and Rory

Barbarian trio v Richmond: they all scored – Richard Carter, Marc Breeze and Jamie Davies.

Coach Simon King brought good young talent to the club.

Gallagher returned, but Christian Richards retired injured, Aaron Bray went to France and Marc Breeze to the Blues. In too came Evan Yardley (under-16/18 cap and Academy hooker) and prop Chris John (Treorchy).

Gareth Harvey, an under-18 cap, also arrived, but injury forced the splendid Andrew Fisher into retirement, while Ben John, Sam Williams, Will Price and James King became Ospreys. David Pritchard played in 25 league matches with Carter, Jamie and Howard Thomas (from Llandovery) on 24. Ian Moore had a broken arm and missed seven matches.

Richard Carter (13) and David Pritchard (10) were the leading league try-scorers. Carter scored a hat-trick in a 48-29 win over Llanelli and there were eight try-scorers in the 11-try walloping of Cross Keys by 75-29 with Jamie scoring 25 points from a try and 10 conversions. He also scored 25 against Newport in which

Jamie Davies sends out a scoring pass against Cardiff.

136

two penalty tries were recorded and when Richard Morris was making his 500th appearance.

There was a double over Neath as a Rhyddian Gierat try helped the away win and Ricky Thomas grabbed the try in the home victory as Jamie kicked 11 points in each match. The win at the Gnoll was Aberavon's first there since Boxing Day 1984. There was a run of seven wins and a draw early season and the last six were also won, while Aberavon were just three points off capturing the title, completing a remarkable double over title-winners Pontypridd.

The League results took the club to a fine third place: P 26, W 19, D 1, L 6. Jamie Davies topped the whole league with 307 pts., 350 overall. The play-off for 2nd/3rd saw Aberavon lose to Llanelli 26-40 at Parc y Scarlets. Morgan Allen (Ospreys) and Neil White scored tries and Craig Evans kicked 16 points.

The Cup had seen Bargoed of Division 1 East visit and pull off a surprising, yet deserved, win by 17-15 as part of their 'rise'. In friendlies, Carter scored four tries against Moseley and Steve Davies, out almost the whole season with injury, ran in three against the Leinster Sea Lions.

The GB/Irish Cup, one of the plethora of efforts to add fixtures and enthuse fans, was 'a bridge too far', with losses to London Welsh 19-27, Llanelli 22-47 and Melrose 8-9 before defeating Esher 40-14. Jamie Davies and Chris Davies played for the Barbarians against the South of Scotland and Simon King coached a Welsh Premiership XV against Georgia at Bridgend with Carter, Jamie, Chris and Will Taylor taking part.

At the end of the season, Taylor, James Donovan, Gallagher and Daryl Harvey left, but the biggest shock was that coach Nicky Lloyd was not offered an extension to his contract. Chris Gittins came out of retirement to play four games (258 in all), Richard Morris reached 508 appearances with Jamie 383, Lloyd Howell 305, Moore 255, Paul Bamsey 232 and Carter 205.

Jamie had now scored 3,862 points, of which 3,133 were in the league – both club records – but his 639 league points while at Aberavon Quins took his league figures to an all-time Welsh record. He had scored 98 tries for Aberavon, of which 73 were in the league, and with 35 in the league at Aberavon Quins, 108 overall.

Morris extended the club record to 154 tries while Carter had 132, Liam Gadd 53 (343 pts) and Richard Thomas 50.

Sam Williams was a surprising choice for captain in 2012-13: not only young, but still fighting for a starting place. It added too much pressure on this promising player and he played only 10 Premiership fixtures. After 13 matches Aberavon had only beaten Bedwas (25-22). However, they had

Scrum half David Pritchard on the burst.

not shed huge amounts and the reappearance of David Pritchard, after foot operations, was the turning point. He played in all the last nine games and Aberavon won seven, including home to Cardiff (11-3) and away to Neath (13-12).

Jamie Davies and Craig Evans combined well, with the latter being one of the club's most popular players and scoring 99 league points. The presence of Ian Moore, Lee Purnell (Gilfach Goch) and hooker Ieuan Davies (an under-18 cap from Treorchy, via Cardiff) tightened the pack, though props Tony Edwards and Lloyd Howell were injured, but the outstanding Rowan Jenkins and Andrew Clatworthy (back from Swansea) took the latter roles.

Craig Warlow emerged as a likeable, quiet and thoughtful backs coach but Richard Morris was never in favour and for the first time in 16 seasons failed to score a try. Ben Thomas returned from Bridgend and played in all 22 league matches with Craig Evans, Clatworthy and Moore 21 each. Other new faces included the exciting and entertaining Stefan Andrews (Tonmawr), Jonny Phillips (Bridgend Athletic), Joe Tomalin-Reeves (Academy/Swansea), Matthew Jenkins (an Academy forward converted to centre) and Joe Heatley (Tondu).

Injuries kept out Danny Davies (broken ankle), Darryl Thomas (knee), Howard Thomas and Ricky Thomas, while the coaches cast out the talented Liam Gadd, who had scored 343 points in 199 games. It was the end for popular Nathan Strong, with injury, after 63 appearances and for the amiable

Steve 'Stella' Davies (26 tries in 78 matches). Aberavon finished 9th out of 12 but bottom club Swansea was not relegated: gosh!

In the Cup, Aberavon defeated Whitland 42-0 away; Beddau 44-6 (with a 100th club try for Jamie Davies in his tally of 20 points) and then Swansea, 23-16 away. However, they lost the semi-final 22-27 to Neath at St Helen's, despite 17 points by Jamie and a Matthew Jenkins try. The unloved GB/Irish Cup was another total disaster, losing to Rotherham 21-25 and 7-49; Munster 'A' 11-19 and 14-18 and Plymouth Albion 20-21 and 0-59.

Ex-Wales centre Mark Taylor was employed as a defence coach, while Jamie now tallied 411 matches. He scored 192 points overall. It was a huge mistake to show Craig Evans 'the door' to Carmarthen Quins, after 49 games and 173 points. Morris had played 528 matches and scored 154 tries; Carter 140 tries in 228 matches and the first player from any club to score 100 Premiership tries, while other high appearances tallies came from Howell (308), the outstanding Moore (284) and Bamsey (251). The record was: P 22, W 8, D 1, L 13, for 9th.

Paul Williams' recalls some of the year's clashes: *"The Cup win at Whitland was in itself not a particularly significant result, but it did have the effect of restoring some confidence during a season that had gone from bad to worse.*

"The 41-39 win over Cross Keys came despite trailing 32-7 after 50 minutes, but Aberavon closed it to 39-38 and thought it would be two losing bonus points. Then Keys conceded a penalty and Jamie banged it over from wide on the touchline with the last kick of the match.

"The Cup semi-final against Neath was lost due to poor decision-making that potentially cost Aberavon the match, but Carter was cynically obstructed when chasing a kick that was rolling over the line in the second half. Referee Sean Brickell awarded a penalty and yellow-carded perpetrator Dafydd Howells, but referee's assessor Nigel Whitehouse later said it should have been a penalty try and a red card.

"I didn't think Carter would have got there before the ball rolled dead, but others disagreed. Howells' card meant Neath were down to 13 as Chris Morgans was also binned, but Chris Davies asked Jamie to go for goal from way out on the line. The kick narrowly missed, when probably we should have opted for a scrum or lineout with Neath two men short.

"The 33-22 victory over Bridgend in the last league game saw Stefan Andrews score an amazing solo try that was voted "Try of the Season" at the WRU Premiership Awards Night."

The scoreboard at the dressing-room end had been operated by various Supporters' Club Committee members, but that committee was 'wound up' around 1999. Paul Williams had worked it many times from 1982 to 1999 and became the regular operator for a number of years until his wife,

Elaine, took over from 2003 to May 2013. Paul had become the Programme Editor. A new electronic scoreboard was introduced from August 2013.

In season 2013-14 Aberavon met sadness, dreadful form and changes in coaches, captain and squad. Outstanding servants retired and right at the finish, it was Ian Moore – a legend in his own lifetime – who made grown men, including one Howard Evans, cry with joy.

Newcomers had included Mike Powell (Bridgend Ath); Aaron Jones (Tata); Paul Smithson (Tondu); the much-travelled Craig Everett; Chris Morgans back from Neath and Andrew Collins (Tata). The Premiership began with a win over Newport with Paul Yardley as forwards coach, since Chris Gittins had left. Backs coach Craig Warlow was dismissed on October 27 and within 10 days head coach Simon King also went, with Aberavon in bottom place.

Simon had taken the 'Wizards' to their highest-ever position of third in the Premiership and to a Cup final, being in charge of 236 games (W 139, D 8, L 89). He also had brought on some good young players and had probably the best record of an Aberavon coach in the Premiership. As Kevin Hopkins once said, though, *"Four seasons is enough for a coach at any club."*

Recruitment was poor and the future looked black for the 'Blood and Blacks'. Just before Simon left, former centre Barry Maddocks was appointed backs coach, and Aberavon then turned to former hooker Jason Hyatt, who had coached Tonmawr, Swansea and Waunarlwydd, as the new head coach.

Hyatt and Maddocks began with a win over Bridgend. Aberavon played with no real confidence, but it was obvious the players were responding to the new pairing. It was no coincidence that yet again the four Ospreys clubs were in the bottom four positions, yet the region seemed never to query their hand – whether helping(?) or hindering – in the situation.

A defeat at Cardiff saw the finish for Darryl Thomas as injury closed his career. He played 196 times and was beloved by teammates and supporters alike. 'Trigger' was a massive loss, but he eventually became the Talbot groundsman while also coaching at Baglan.

Hyatt gave the captaincy to Ian Moore and in came a new wing, Jay Baker (Cwmavon), but injury reduced him to three league games. Then the coaches pulled a master stroke in bringing in No. 8 Tim Duncan and ex-Carmarthen Quins centre Rheon James, both on a month's loan from Cornish Pirates. Rheon notched a try to help defeat Swansea and Tim's try saw off Newport.

The popular Darren Ryan returned from Cardiff and the experienced Ceiron Thomas was also recruited from the capital: but then came disaster, as Jamie Davies, a replacement against Cross Keys, dislocated an elbow and his career was over. Pritchard was back, fighting operations and ring-rusty,

Jamie Davies' 100th try as he gets a pat from Rob Downes of Beddau.

Flanker Chris Davies races over in the Cup against Beddau.

Jason Hyatt and Barry Maddocks were to become club coaches.

but he was a talisman. Against Llanelli, Ceiron broke a wrist and in stepped young Aaron Jones for the game of his life with two solo tries and two conversions as Aberavon won 22-11.

Table-toppers Pontypridd came and led 27-26 with seconds remaining, when Stefan Andrews caught a kick in front of the grandstand and emergency full back Richard Carter called for it, stunning friend and foe alike with a sensational dropped goal. Aberavon lost 10-42 at Pontypridd three days later and then drew 10-10 at Llandovery where they were forced to give teenager Aaron Grabham, son of Barry, a debut on the wing with Andrew Collins pressed into service as fly half. They had no kicker, though Richard Thomas tried, but failed.

Swansea then thrashed Aberavon 46-0 though the refereeing left more than a little to be desired. Neath came on Easter Monday and won 27-10, with Aaron Jones breaking his leg very badly and having his career cut short. Aberavon needed one point for safety and were home to second-placed Carmarthen Quins, while Swansea had to take five points against Neath.

No Aberavon supporter had expected Neath to turn up. They didn't and Swansea smashed them, while Quins looked good until Phillips, Andrews and Matthew Jenkins scored first-half tries. It still looked likely that Quins would win, but Aberavon needed that bonus point. Then, after 44 minutes, skipper Moore not only scored his first try for seven years, but probably the most important in the club's history.

Darren Ryan, with a broken arm, gave his all, and Lee Evans, loaned by Llandovery, scored a fifth try that Nic Damjanovic, on permit from Trebanos, converted. That took Aberavon to 10th, over Neath with Swansea relegated. Meanwhile, the Quins scored again and again to win 37-31. So the table ended with: P 22, W 7, D 1, L 14 and Aberavon's 37 tries were the lowest in the division.

Hyatt was in charge for the Cup run, beating Bridgend 21-19; Narberth 19-6 (away) and Carmarthen Quins 26-22, but in the semi at Bridgend, Pontypridd blasted the 'Wizards' out by 32-3.

The GB/Irish Cup began under Simon King, winning qualifying games over Swansea 15-8 and Bridgend 35-26, though Aberavon (so the side was named!) continued with a 31-17 win at Gala and then a large hole appeared in the pitch near halfway, just when Aberavon had fought back to 20-24 at home to Bristol with 10 minutes remaining.

Aberavon, with few club players in the side, fell 22-41 to Leeds Carnegie and Bristol returned to win 78-0. Ever wanted the pitch to open up and..? It became worse as trips to Leeds and Bristol (0-72 and 8-64) meant Aberavon conceded 214 points in three games: yet they rallied to defeat Gala 11-9. The GB/Irish Cup, then, was an embarrassment, with 16 Ospreys and Academy players 'imposed', of whom 14 were worse than bad – and then there was Aisea Natoga....! Only prop Nicky Thomas was exempt from criticism.

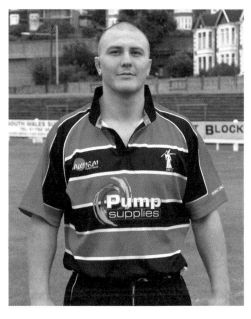

Daryll 'Trigger' Thomas.

David Pritchard missed 19 of the 22 games after another operation; Sam Williams most of the season with a shoulder injury; Lloyd Howell retired after four games (312 overall); Howard Thomas left and a frustrated Liam Gadd joined Bedwas, while injury ruled out Ricky Thomas.

Richard Thomas joined Llanelli after good service with 172 games and 61 tries; Joe Heatley and Paul Smithson returned to Tondu; Anthony Edwards succumbed to injury after 202 games and joined Lloyd Howell in retirement, while Rhyddian Gierat joined Bridgend. Carter took his appearances to 251 and tries to 150; Neil White had played 213 games and skipper Moore was on 313.

Ben Thomas was the only player to appear in all 22 league games with Rowan Jenkins 21 and Gavin Ronan and Chris Davies 20. Paul Bamsey, an outstanding servant, retired after 260 games and Richard Morris also retired after 540 games and a club record of 155 tries.

Jamie Davies scored only 76 points and retired after 429 games with a league record of 3,261 points (73t, 545c, 595p, 7dg) and a club record of 4,130 points (101t, 770c, 688p, 7dg). With his 639 points at Aberavon Quins, his full league total was a staggering 3,900 points (108t, 654c, 676p, 8dg). Genuinely legendary, and with a legendary, modest genuineness.

Chris O'Callaghan reflected: *'Jamie was the best £5,000 Aberavon have ever spent. We shouldn't have had to pay that, as he had been an Aberavon Youth player, but the WRU district rep was from Aberavon Quins at that time and they leaned on the Union.*

"The boy was a phenomenon and if he were not so unassuming and just had a bit more self-confidence he could have had a great career at a much higher level. Thankfully for Aberavon, he didn't. However, what he's achieved will never be bettered."

That crucial clash with the Quins, though, was a special afternoon. Its atmosphere and aftermath are captured here by Paul Williams, who writes on 'The Last Day':

"April 26th 2014. Just another Saturday. Or maybe not. The nerves started to jangle early as I went about my usual Saturday morning business like an automaton, with my mind on other things. On one other thing, actually – the quest for that elusive bonus-point. Failure to get it wasn't an option, and the mind's eye wandered through scenarios that were all about who might score the tries that would rescue my beloved Wizards.

"I imagined Jonny Phillips racing away chasing one of his kicks ahead, Jay Baker thundering down the touchline, Stef Andrews weaving his magic, Matthew Jenkins cutting one of those great angles, Nathan Brown charging head-down for the posts, 'Pritch' bursting clean through from a lineout...

Joining Ceiron and Jamie amongst the walking-wounded, 'Gav the Goon' was also out, along with any number of others suffering the effects of a hectic late-season schedule. We've had to borrow players to make up the numbers, I thought, and these guys won't be familiar with those around them.

Another try for Leeds (Yorkshire) Carnegie.

The legend: Jamie Davies.

"Fast-forward to half-time. Stef had indeed woven his magic, 'JP' had indeed done his special thing in pursuit of a bouncing kick-ahead, and Matthew had indeed cut a great angle and forced his way through. Job 75% done.

"Aberavon kick off, the Carmarthen forwards secure the ball, but as they attempted to move it out of danger it gets spilled. Onto it like a shot is Darren Ryan, charging away with his usual degree of regard for personal safety (or rather, the lack thereof). Up to within a few yards of the Carmarthen line and back it comes again to one of those guys who wouldn't be familiar with those around him.

"Nic Damjanovic makes light of the situation by slicing through almost to the posts, perfectly setting up a ruck from which one of the Aberavon greats of the modern era, Ian George 'Buddha' Moore, picks up and throws himself across the line to finish the job.

"A tidal wave of emotion washes over all and sundry. Players are running from all parts of the field to congratulate the hero, the noise echoing through the stand threatens to lift the roof, the past-players reunion and the match sponsors crazy with delight and suddenly, after Nic has put over the conversion, the game may as well be over from an Aberavon viewpoint. Victory or defeat won't matter, although another bonus-point would be nice.

"Fast-forward again to the final minutes. The visitors have all but secured victory, but the Wizards have the last word as another of the 'guest' players, Lee Evans, goes flying in beneath the posts to reduce the margin to just eight points. Nic again sends over the conversion to bring that second bonus-point into range and it is Carmarthen who are eventually relieved to kick for touch and bring down the curtain on a remarkable match.

"Looking back, much of it seems a blur. The post-match socialising gathers pace with a happy crowd augmented by the Former Players' Association and we have the unusual spectacle of a rugby match ending with both camps more than happy with their day's work.

"The clubhouse is bouncing; the staff are concerned that we'll run out of beer and the overall atmosphere is one of all-pervading delight. People are trading tales of the emotional roller-coaster they've just experienced, and even that great clubman Richard Morris admits to shedding a tear or two of joy at the sight of 'Buddha' crashing over for his try.

'And that is why we support the Wizards, and why we shall continue to support them come what may, and why we would have continued to support them even if The Last Day hadn't unfolded the way it did. Aberavon RFC is like a family, but bigger: supporters, staff and players all pulling in one direction for the good of the club. May it ever remain that way." Just so!

Season 2014-15 saw Ian Moore captain again, and for 'Buddah' it was also the season when he did represent the Barbarians, having been pulled out for an important club game two years before. He played against the Combined Services on November 11, and as usual, hordes of 'Wizards' were present to rejoice with him.

It was a tough season with seven of the opening eight league matches lost and the sole win at Bedwas (31-24), where Nic Damjanovic scored 18 points. Later on, there were seven successive wins, which included gaining two penalty tries at Cardiff. Tries were hard to come by, though, and the tally of 42 was just higher than bottom club Newport, who – surprise, surprise – were not relegated!

Aberavon finished 7th out of 12 (P 22, W 10, L 12) and much was due to the signing from Poneke RFC in New Zealand of fly half Cameron Clement, whose 91 points in 11 matches were extremely valuable. Cameron's father, Mike, had been an Aberavon player and his uncle Tony was a Wales cap and Lion. While Moore never played a bad game, Rowan Jenkins and David Pritchard were probably the best Premiership players in their positions.

New signings included Ryan Harford from Cardiff, Kristian Corbisiero and Ben Davies. Howard Thomas returned, but suffered injury as did Ricky Thomas, while the talented Jonny Phillips was fit for only one league match. 'Outgoings' included Gavin Ronan, Evan Yardley, Darren Ryan and Nic Damjanovic.

At the end of the season, Ben Thomas moved to Cardiff, Ceiron Thomas to Llangennech, Chris Morgans back to Neath and Neil White, a fine clubman, to Swansea. Darren Ryan had reached 157 matches with 141 points and Neil White had played 235 matches.

Nicky Thomas of the Ospreys was a splendid and extremely popular prop, who played 21 games before signing for Gloucester, while Matthew Jarvis (Ealing Trailfinders) had two loan games. Andrew Gwynne retired, while Academy players Adam Beard, Joe Gage and Morgan Williams (all Under-20 caps) played much of the season and Sam Williams and Will Price returned after their Ospreys contracts ended.

Jamie Davies and Richard Morris went onto the coaching staff; Rob Hill was forwards coach and former Wales cap Andy Williams was backs coach for several months and played in two matches. Former prop Colin Noon was later brought in as scrummaging coach.

A friendly brought a good 27-24 win over Cornish Pirates, but the Cup ended 10-11 at Newport. The GB/Irish Cup saw qualifying wins over Neath (25-10) and Bridgend (20-19 away with a last-gasp Ceiron Thomas drop goal). Then, Ulster 'A' were beaten 18-14, but losses came to Rotherham Titans (15-37 and 14-42); Yorkshire Carnegie (0-85 and 32-43) and Ulster 'A' (12-25 away).

The greatest try – skipper Ian Moore steers Aberavon from relegation against Carmarthen Quins.

Aberavon's squad 2013-14: captain Ian Moore, head coach Jason Hyatt.

Richard Carter became the highest-ever try-scorer in Premiership rugby and the semi-pro era. Ben Thomas and Rowan Jenkins played all 22 league games with Pritchard and Ieuan Davies on 21. Carter (273 games) had taken his try-count to 153, two behind the record of Morris, while Moore reached 336 appearances.

Former 'Wizard', Mike Nicholas, brought out a book titled *'From Swn-y-Mor to Seattle'*. 'Nicko' had been a boyhood Aberavon fan and stood on the terraces with Richard Burton before captaining his school rugby team as they remained unbeaten for three years. He played for Aberavon BC, Aberavon Quins, Aberavon Green Stars and finally, Aberavon, before joining Warrington RL with great success in 1972 and eventually becoming a force for rugby league in and for Wales.

For his services to rugby and business in the area, Chairman Andrew John was made Freeman of Neath and Port Talbot in 2014, flanked by comedians Max Boyce and Colin Price: some front row! Meanwhile, the death of Trevor Lloyd, scrum half for Aberavon, Maesteg, Wales and the 1955 Lions was announced during the season. He was at the time of his death the oldest-surviving Lion.

Ian Moore was again skipper as Aberavon entered the 2015-16 Principality Premiership season with head coach Jason Hyatt having been joined by backs coach Lyndon Lewis, the former Aberavon full back and captain, and more recently the Llandovery head coach. The side was captained on several occasions by Chris Davies, who was also a very efficient Commercial Manager of the club.

The WRU once more made less-than-popular changes, with tries worth six points and all goals two points, though the SWALEC Cup saw it all revert to the old values. Aberavon hardly tasted the latter, as they fell 8-11 in North Wales to RGC 1404 at the first hurdle, having received a bye in Round One. The club almost made the semi-finals of another new Cup, the 'Fosters', which included a 0-0 home draw (so rare these days) with Pontypridd in what was still a very good game.

The Premiership saw the 'Wizards' reach top spot at one time and they recorded the double over Simon King's Cardiff side by 24-6 home and 24-8 away. Richard Carter took his overall try record to 157 (passing Richard Morris as the club's highest-ever). Both David Pritchard and Chris Davies passed 200 appearances while Ian Moore reached 355 and Carter 290, having tallied 796 points. Aberavon ended up 5th in the division with: P 22, W 13, D 2, L 7.

New faces included utility back Steffan Williams; scrum half Jacob Flynn; young forwards Rhys Forse, Jacob Blackmore, Mike Burgess and James Ratti; James Garland rejoined from Llandovery (being top scorer with 121 points) and the pack included Ben Jones and Jon Thomas from Bridgend.

Andrew John, Freeman of the Borough, 2014.

Will Price missed almost the whole season with injury, while prop Rowan Jenkins played in every league match (22) and Pritchard, Chris Davies and Jon Thomas all appeared in 21.

Jay Baker and Stefan Andrews were outstanding wings and centre Joe Thomas came from the Ospreys Academy. Morgan Williams played for Wales 7s while Adam Beard, Joe Gage and Joe Thomas all played for Wales Under-20s. At the end of the season forwards coach Colin Noon finished and popular conditioning coach Dan Cunningham moved on. Team manager Steve Jones, paramedic Richard Hook and head baggage man David Beaton continued to give great service, along with numerous other backroom staff.

It was 'as you were' for 2016-17 as Jason Hyatt and Lyndon Lewis remained coaches with Ian Moore as captain, but the club lost two of its old international players when first Emlyn Davies and David Thomas passed away, then 1964-65 centre and captain Brian Jones followed. Further sadness but again, great memories were evoked when on May 9, 2017, the splendid international wing John Collins, whose try gave Wales a win over the 1958 Australians, also died.

In came Matthew Jacobs (Llandovery), Rheon James (Cornish Pirates), Luke Joseph (Coventry) and former player Howard Thomas as a fine conditioning coach. Aberavon temporarily lost the brilliant Stef Andrews, who played for Wales at Sevens, while the Ospreys used Rowan Jenkins, Jay Baker, Joe Thomas, Adam Beard and James Ratti and occasionally Joe Tomalin-Reeves and Lee Purnell, with splendid prop Alex Jeffries an Osprey, though almost a regular with the club. In February, Cameron Clement left for a year in Australia.

The Premiership now had 16 clubs with 15 games played in the first part of the season – eight home and seven away – and Aberavon finished top, playing exciting and adventurous rugby. The league then split into two with eight clubs each, so there were now seven more games to play: Aberavon having three home and four away. Before that the 'Wizards' missed out on the Fosters Cup semi-finals by one point and then, with a weakened team, crashed out of the Welsh Cup 10-34 at home to holders Llandovery at the very first hurdle.

Record try-man Richard Carter.

The first seven league games were won before a home loss to Cardiff, and other defeats followed at Pontypridd and Newport with a draw at Bedwas, but the first round of 15 games had brought 11 wins and top place, including beating Neath 59-18 at home on Boxing Day and winning by 52-14 at Bridgend five days later. Andrews scored three tries against Neath and David Griggs (Tata) touched down three in the Fosters Cup at home to Cardiff.

After playing his 300th match, away to Cross Keys, and having scored a club record of 163 tries, Richard Carter was sacked, while Andrew Clatworthy went to Moriston in semi-retirement. Crazily, on January 29 there were only three home matches remaining in the next round of the Top Eight as Aberavon started the second part of the Premiership.

While the community awaited nervously the outcome of the latest ups and downs of the now-Tata Steelworks, the club spent weeks 'unemployed' due to the baffling and counter-productive WRU fixture list. The 'Wizards' restarted badly with a loss

Current Aberavon coaches Jason Hyatt and Lyndon Lewis.

at Ebbw Vale, but though often deprived of Steff Andrews (Wales 7s) and Jay Baker, Rowan Jenkins and Alex Jeffries (all Ospreys), they convincingly beat RGC and Pontypridd at home, with Baker grabbing a hat-trick of tries in the latter game.

More wins came away to Llandovery and Carmarthen Quins and though they narrowly lost at Merthyr, Aberavon defeated Bedwas 28-9 at home to secure a further home match against the same club in the Premiership semi-final play-off. Another splendid match saw Aberavon edge out a battling Bedwas side by 31-24 as the Wizards lasted the distance better, though Steve Law's side battled hard. James Garland controlled it well, though Andrews was away playing Sevens. It was Ben Davies who scored a vital fourth Aberavon try.

Jason Hyatt then called the coin correctly and the 'Wizards' were thus home in the final to Merthyr. There they led twice, but there were dropped passes at crucial times and some splendid Merthyr covering that was matched by tremendous Aberavon defence, but it fell just short, with the Ironmen gaining a 22-18 win in a good advert for Premiership rugby.

Lee Purnell (broken arm) and Joe Gage (in a wheelchair) watched as Joe Tomalin-Reeves left, badly shaken, at half-time. Jay Baker was amazingly exciting and it was well worth flying him home in the early hours from

Andrew John celebrates a vital try by Ben Davies.

an emergency call-up for Ospreys cover in Ireland. Aberavon were leading 11-9 with only eight minutes remaining, but it was not to be.

It was goodbye to the legend – Ian Moore – and also to Stefan Andrews (transferring to Merthyr), Nathan Brown, Matthew Jacobs and Chris Davies (all retiring) and to Matthew Jenkins and Gareth Harvey (both transferring).

As the season ended the WRU staged a Premiership Sevens tournament at Parc y Scarlets with Aberavon beating Ebbw Vale 28-19; Pontypridd 29-12 and Cross Keys 31-19 before losing 24-33 to Llandovery in the final. Jacob Flynn then travelled with Wales to a Sevens tournament in Russia, while at the WRU's Premiership Awards, Jason Hyatt received Coach of the Season and Steve Jones well merited the Unsung Hero Award.

May there be many more as deserving – and as rewarded – on and off the field, and may Aberavon RFC continue to cast a Wizard's spell over the faithful at the Talbot Athletic Ground and beyond as they move on towards completing a century and a half of rugby football: usually fun, often fraught, frequently frantic, occasionally fantastic – but all unfailingly memorable.

Thanks for those memories.....

APPENDIX 1

Club Captains:

1876-77 Richard Cook Jenkins
1877-78 to 1880-81 no records
1881-82 Dr. Jack H. Davies
1882-86 Club disbanded
1886-87 to 1892-93 Ivor Griffiths
   (7 seasons)
1893-94 Jack A. Harries
1894-95 Harry John
1895-96 Ivor Griffiths
1896-97 Evan Jones
1897-98 Evan Jones
1898-99 Dan Jones
1899-1900 Dan Jones
1900-01 Alfred Brice
1901-02 Alfred Brice
1902-03 Tim Madden
1903-04 George Vickery
1904-05 George Vickery
1905-06 Tom Thomas
1906-07 Will Gregory
1907-08 Will Jones
1908-09 William R. Thomas
1909-10 E. Pugh
1910-11 Rees Richards
1911-12 Jim Donovan
1912-13 Rees Richards
1913-14 Will Hopkins
1914-15 Will Hopkins
1915-16 to 1918-19 (War years)
1919-20 Will Hopkins
1920-21 Will Hopkins
1921-22 Jim Jones
1922-23 Jim Jones
1923-24 Bob Randall
1924-25 Will J. ('Noisy') Thomas
1925-26 William John Hopkins

1926-27 Jack Jeremy
1927-28 David Williams
1928-29 Miah McGrath
1929-30 Miah McGrath
1930-31 E.M. ('Ned') Jenkins
1931-32 Cyril Griffiths
1932-33 E.M. ('Ned') Jenkins
1933-34 E.M. ('Ned') Jenkins
1934-35 Tommy Owen James
1935-36 John H. (Jack) Thomas
1936-37 Walter E. Vickery
1937-38 George Davies
1938-39 George Davies
1939-40 Haydn Williams
1940-41 to 1944-45 (War years)
1945-46 Walter E. Vickery
1946-47 David M. James
1947-48 Will Thomas
1948-49 Joe Drew
1949-50 Emlyn Davies
1950-51 John Evans
1951-52 Denzil Jones
1952-53 Denzil Jones
1953-54 Merlin Williams
1954-55 Roy Bish
1955-56 Cliff Ashton
1956-57 Cliff Ashton
1957-58 Tony O'Connor
1958-59 Len Cunningham
1959-60 Len Cunningham
1960-61 Rory O'Connor
1961-62 Rory O'Connor
1962-63 Len Cunningham
1963-64 Phil Morgan
1964-65 Brian Jones
1965-66 Max Wiltshire

1966-67 Max Wiltshire
1967-68 Cyril Jones
1968-69 Morton Howells
1969-70 Billy Mainwaring
1970-71 Billy Mainwaring
1971-72 Ian Hall

1972-73 Morton Howells
1973-74 Morton Howells
1974-75 Morton Howells
1975-76 Richie Davies
1976-77 Clive Shell
1977-78 Clive Shell

Vintage issues & Modern Wizards programmes featuring Paul Bamsey, Richard Carter and Dan Hawkins.

1978-79 Clive Shell

1979-80 Billy James

1980-81 Billy James

1981-82 Allan Martin

1982-83 Adrian Owen

1983-84 Adrian Owen

1984-85 Billy James

1985-86 Ray Giles

1986-87 Ray Giles

1987-88 Ray Giles/Billy James

1988-89 Billy James/Gary Matthews

1989-90 Gary Matthews

1990-91 Ray Giles

1991-92 Anthony Woodward

1992-93 Lyndon Lewis

1993-94 John Jardine

1994-95 Brian Shenton

1995-96 Brian Shenton

1996-97 Colin Laity

1997-98 Colin Laity

1998-99 Justin Hughes

1999-2000 Mark Evans

2000-01 Daniel Hawkins

2001-02 Steve Rees

2002-03 Chris Gittins

2003-04 Chris Gittins

2004-05 Dafydd Owen

2005-06 Chris Gittins

2006-07 Chris Gittins

2007-08 Ian Moore

2008-09 Ian Moore

2009-10 Ian Moore

2010-11 Chris Davies

2011-12 Chris Davies

2012-13 Sam Williams

2013-14 Andrew Clatworthy

2014-15 Ian Moore

2015-16 Ian Moore

2016-17 Ian Moore

Chairmen:

1886-87 F. G. Jenkins

1887-88 F.W. Jenkins

1899-1900 Dr. Jack Davies

1900-01 F. G. Jenkins

1901-02 F. G. Jenkins

1902-03 F. G. Jenkins

1904-04 F. G. Jenkins

1905-06 F. G. Jenkins

1906-07 F. G. Jenkins

1907-08 Lewis M. Thomas

1908-09 Lewis M. Thomas

1909-10 Lewis M. Thomas

1910-11 Lewis M. Thomas

1911-12 Lewis M. Thomas

1912-13 Lewis M. Thomas

1913-14 Lewis M. Thomas

1919-20 Lewis M. Thomas

1920-21 Lewis M. Thomas

1921-22 Willie R. Thomas

1922-23 Willie R. Thomas

1923-24 Willie R. Thomas

1924-25 Willie R. Thomas

1925-26 Willie R. Thomas

1926-27 Willie R. Thomas

1927-28 Willie R. Thomas

1928-29 Willie R. Thomas

1929-30 Willie R. Thomas

1930-31 Willie R. Thomas

1931-32 Willie R. Thomas

1932-33 Willie R. Thomas

1933-34 Willie R. Thomas

1934-35 Willie R. Thomas

1935-36 Willie R. Thomas

1936-37 Willie R. Thomas

1937-38 Willie R. Thomas

1938-39 Willie R. Thomas

1939-40 Willie R. Thomas	1973-74 George Davies
1945-46 Willie R. Thomas	1974-75 George Davies
1946-47 Willie R. Thomas	1975-76 Brian Tashara
1947-48 Willie R. Thomas	1976-77 George Davies
1948-49 Willie R. Thomas	1977-78 George Davies
1949-50 Willie R. Thomas	1978-79 Ross Richards
1950-51 Willie R. Thomas	1979-80 Ross Richards
1951-52 Willie R. Thomas	1980-81 Frank Williams
1952-53 Willie R. Thomas	1981-82 Frank Williams
1953-54 Willie R. Thomas	1982-83 Hywel Thomas
1954-55 Willie R. Thomas	1983-84 Hywel Thomas
1955-56 Willie R. Thomas	1984-85 Ken Jones
1956-57 Willie R. Thomas	1985-86 Ken Jones
1957-58 Lord Heycock	1986-87 Emlyn Davies
1958-59 Lord Heycock	1987-88 Phil Morgan
1959-60 Lord Heycock	1988-89 Phil Morgan
1960-61 Lord Heycock	1989-90 Morton Howells
1961-62 Lord Heycock	1990-91 Morton Howells
1962-63 Lord Heycock	1991-92 Dr Keith James
1963-64 Lord Heycock	1992-93 Dr Keith James
1964-65 Lord Heycock	1993-94 Haldon Lodwig
1965-66 Lord Heycock	1994-95 Peter Stevens
1966-67 Lord Heycock	1995-96 Peter Stevens
1967-68 Lord Heycock	1996-97 David L. Thomas
1968-69 Lord Heycock	1997-98 David L. Thomas
1969-70 Lord Heycock	1998-99 David Condon
1970-71 Lord Heycock	
1971-72 Lord Heycock	(The role of Chairman ended at that
1972-73 George Davies	point.)

Players of the Year:

1967 – Bobby Wanbon	1975 – Richie Davies
1968 – Cyril Jones	1976 – Phil Clarke
1969 – Ceri Jones	1977 – Billy Mainwaring
1970 – Mike Nicholas	1978 – Barry Lewis
1971 – Morton Howells	1979 – Wynford Lewis
1972 – Clive Shell	1980 – Bernard Thomas
1973 – Allan Martin	1981 – Adrian Owen
1974 – John Bevan	1982 – Adrian Owen

1983 – Kevin James
1984 – Mike Edwards
1985 – Ray Giles
1986 – Ray Giles
1987 – Ray Giles
1988 – Tim Fauvel
1989 – Gary Matthews
1990 – Kevin George
1991 – Matthew McCarthy
1992 – Anthony Dragone
1993 – Mark Evans
1994 – Brian Shenton
1995 – Stephen Ford
1996 – Colin Laity
1997 – Paul Clapham
1998 – Richard Morris
1999 – Justin Hughes
2000 – Chris Kinsey

2001 – Richard Morris
2002 – Andrew Thomas
2003 – Richard Morris
2004 – Richard Morris
2005 – Ian Moore
2006 – Jamie Davies
2007 – Darren Ryan
2008 – Richard Carter
2009 – Chris Davies
2010 – Marc Breeze
2011 – Ian Moore
2012 – David Pritchard
2013 – Ian Moore
2014 – Ian Moore
2015 – Rowan Jenkins
2016 – Joe Tomalin-Reeves
2017 – Will Price

Joe Tomalin-Reeves (2016 Player of the Year) with wing Stef Andrews.

James Garland, fly half and captain 2017-18.

Clubmen of the Year:

1980 – Adrian Owen
1981 – Bernard Thomas
1982 – Mike Edwards
1983 – Les Keen
1984 – Gary Matthews
1985 – Jeff Jenkins
1986 – Paul Knight
1987 – Paul Yardley
1988 – Nigel Spender
1989 – Les Keen
1990 – Lyndon Lewis
1991 – Graham Evans
1992 – John Jardine
1993 – Dylan Davies
1994 – Phil Hamley
1995 – Chris Kinsey
1996 – Chris Kinsey
1997 – Mavis Ackery
1998 – Richard Diplock

1999 – Richard Lewis
2000 – Steve Jones
2001 – Chris O'Callaghan
2002 – Andrew John
2003 – Richard Morris
2004 – Mike Harris
2005 – Andrew & Mair John
2006 – Jeff Preece & Dennis Morgan
2007 – Mike Harris
2008 – Ian Moore
2009 – Ian Moore
2010 – Chris Gittins
2011 – Paul Breeze
2012 – Ian Moore
2013 – Gareth Gange
2014 – Ian Moore
2015 – Ian Moore
2016 – Chris Davies
2017 – Chris Davies

Most Promising Players of the Year:

1991 – Andrew Graham
1992 – Dean Griffiths
1993 – Chris Kinsey
1994 – Lee Williams
1995 – Paul Williams
1996 – Steve Pearce
1997 – Daran Griffiths
1998 – Chris Lewis
1999 – Colin Noon
2000 – Paul Bamsey
2001 – Jamie Davies
2002 – Chris Gittins
2003 – Andrew Clatworthy
2004 – Paul Breeze

2005 – Liam Gadd
2006 – Darryl Thomas
2007 – Chris Morgans
2008 – Chris Morgans
2009 – Ashley Beck
2010 – Gavin Ronan
2011 – Dan Davies
2012 – Gareth Harvey
2013 – Matthew Jenkins
2014 – Jay Baker
2015 – Cameron Clement
2016 – Jay Baker
2017 – Jacob Flynn

Players' Players of the Year:

2005 – Ian Moore
2006 – Jamie Davies
2007 – Darryl Thomas
2008 – Ian Moore
2009 – Darryl Thomas
2010 – Marc Breeze
2011 – Will Price

2012 – Jamie Davies
2013 – Lee Purnell
2014 – Ben Thomas
2015 – Rowan Jenkins
2016 – Joe Tomalin-Reeves
2017 – Joe Tomalin-Reeves

Young Players of the Year (The Sean Conneely Award):

2005 – Richard Carter
2006 – Andrew Fisher
2007 – James Jones
2008 – Ashley Beck
2009 – Ashley Beck
2010 – Dan Davies
2011 – Dan Davies

2012 – Gareth Harvey
2013 – Matthew Jenkins
2014 – Aaron Jones
2015 – Joe Tomalin-Reeves
2016 – Joe Gage
2017 – Jacob Flynn

Merlin Man-of-the-Match Award (Supporters' Club):

2005 – Ian Moore
2006 – Jamie Davies
2007 – Darren Ryan
2008 – Ian Moore
2009 – Ashley Beck
2010 – David Pritchard
2011 – Ian Moore

2012 – David Pritchard
2013 – Ian Moore
2014 – Ian Moore
2015 – David Pritchard
2016 – Joe Tomalin-Reeves
2017 – Joe Tomalin-Reeves

APPENDIX 2

THE WALK: by Chris O'Callaghan

From 'The Guv'nor' Series – September 17th, 2003

Memory is a terrible thing, it plays tricks on you. I can remember watching my first game at Aberavon, but I can't remember the result. I can remember the names of Kel Coslett, Len Cunningham, Cliff Ashton, Peter Jones and the two O'Connors but I can't remember whether they played, or who the opponents were. I can remember that the day had been a lovely one, that the night was cold and dry and I can still smell the smells and I remember "The Walk."

Few people had cars, taxis were only something my uncle from America arrived in and we were too tight to catch the bus. So we walked. Big men in big coats looking like Chicago wise boys from the South Side, all of whom had played for Abercrombie, Aberavon's most feared opponents (or so my grandfather Stan would have me believe). One little boy, flanked by three giants, all walking "The Walk."

Right into Pendarvis Terrace, past St Paul's and the Forward Movement – Christians onward marching. A sideways glance at Lennie The Ritz doing more to promote the onset of Smoker's Cough with greater sales of single untipped cigarettes than all of the Virginia tobacco fields and BAT industries put together. Forward, always moving forward: past 'The Greeks' – a tonsorial artiste par excellence, pioneer of the pudding basin cut. Past Mears, purveyors of quality fruit and 'veg' and big in wet fish, the smell of stale beer and Jeyes fluid from the Lib and Burgess Green Hotel way behind us.

Now the stink of the slaughterhouse upon you, squeals and groan of animals who knew that tomorrow was not another day. Now the crowd was swelling, not three and a little boy, more like 300 and all soldiers of Jesus on their way to pay homage at the Church of the Oval Ball. Past the Craddock and The Talbot Hotel, whose inhabitants spilled out with beery breath to join the horde.

A sign of the cross outside St Joe's as the Angelus Bells boom out calling the faithful to prayer – but that night we were fanatical followers of a different faith. Surging forward we were now at Viazanni's, with Eto busily working, and a longing look at Madame Renee's. More disciples emptying the Oddfellows and the Prince of Wales, before a quick sidestep past the old market, a glance at the Lipton's pig and The Home and Colonial Store, before the Cloth Hall Lane, the bridge, level crossing and Chidzoy's brought us to Bethany Square and the final flourish of Station Road.

The faithful were now in full flow, taking Fussells, Selwyn Jenkins and the heady smell of the Chinese onboard, before assaulting Lloyd's Bank, The Grand Hotel and The Plaza Café, where two teas were always 'going cold!' Eagle Street was like the final furlong at Lingfield and the smell of pipe tobacco and 'roll yer owns' was the headiest of all perfumes. I walked that walk many, many times and every time I could feel myself levitating and swelling with pride. The Blood and Blacks were laying waste and slaughtering, and I was going to worship at the shrine.

Years later I walked "The Walk" when I played for the Wizards. Never got a lift, never took a taxi or caught the bus. The feeling was always spiritual. It made me feel ten foot tall. The shouts of encouragement and slaps on the back in Station Road as I marched up sent the hairs on the back of my neck standing on end. I needed no motivation, no pep talk, I lived under the Wizard's spell and I was ready to do his bidding.

Mrs Evelyn Mainwaring:

Evelyn Mainwaring was the best-known club rugby supporter in Wales, though she admitted that before supporting Aberavon her first love had been Taibach RFC.

She had lived near where the M4 was built and so did actor Anthony Hopkins and his parents, so it was no surprise that over her mantle-piece was a photograph of Anthony and one of her sons, Billy Mainwaring. Next to that picture was one of Billy with Ireland and Lions legend Willie-John McBride.

Another son, Bryn, explained that he did not sit with his mother in the grandstand, but opposite on the other side of the field. *"But a friend often says that he hears my mother is at the ground!"* It was hard to miss her and her vocal encouragement.

Mrs. Mainwaring said*: "I started as Miss Evelyn Bamsey, washing the Taibach kit, and all the family were well into rugby. Then, in later years I joined Aberavon."*

When Billy was capped by Wales, Evelyn admitted: *"I asked Brian Price, Billy's Wales lock partner, if he would look after my son at Murrayfield. Brian said that Billy was big enough to look after himself!"*

On one occasion Aberavon were losing to Neath and when she went from her seat in the Gnoll grandstand the Neath announcer said: *"Mrs. Mainwaring is leaving the ground."* The crowd rose to applaud.

She was often worth a few points to the 'Wizards', but maintained that many visiting players were 'nice boys' as well. She lived and died a legend in South Wales rugby circles. Her husband *("Billy's father"*, as she always said) had predeceased her.

Walter Vickery – Red for Wales – The Pull of the Jersey:

In 1999, I went to Port Talbot to see Walter Elias Vickery, who had played four times for Wales (1938 to 1939). He and his father George were unique, as George had actually won an England cap in 1905.

When I met Walter he was aged 90, but his brain was still very active. Living alone (his wife had predeceased him), he greeted me in his Duke Street house with an outstretched left hand.

We went in and he said: *"Do you know why I shook hands left-handed?"* I said I could see that several fingers of his right hand were in a position in the palm of his hand that could not be moved. Indeed, one finger on his left hand was likewise.

He took me through his life. His father had come from Chard in Somerset to Port Talbot where he was a police officer. He had played for Bath and then Aberavon from whom he won a cap against Ireland in Cork four years before Walter was born.

Walter never saw his dad play and at the age of 91, George died, but he had seen his son, a docker, come from Central School in Port Talbot through the ranks of Taibach, British Steel and Cwmavon to join their beloved Aberavon.

Walter played in the Wales pack against England at Cardiff in 1938 and Wales won 14-8. He followed that year against Scotland and Ireland (France were not playing). In 1939, he was in the side at Twickenham. England led 3-0 when Walter suffered a terrible blow to the knee – one he was to suffer for the remainder of his life.

"I played for Wales for the fourth time and Wilf Wooller passed me the ball with 20 yards to go, but my leg had gone and I had already been off the field.

"In those days there were no replacements so I had to come back, but three English players caught me in the corner as I could not get there, running virtually on one leg. But for that I would have scored. I then missed the Scotland and Ireland games."

The War soon followed, but Walter, who skippered Aberavon in 1936-37, returned when hostilities ended to lead them again in 1945-46.

"I was not really fit enough, as I had lost too many good years to the war, and though I had a few war-time games, it was six years before I was back in Aberavon colours.

"I knew I was not right, but had to give it one last go, and yes, despite it all, if I had known how that would have left my fingers and knees in later life, I still would have done it.

"It was all worth it: JUST TO PULL ON THAT RED JERSEY FOR WALES."

Walter showed me a dirty old bandaged boot that he had kept near an outside coal shed and said: *"I wore this one at Twickenham in 1939!"*

In the following year, April 2000, this fine gentleman died, though not before he admitted to playing just one game for Aberavon's deadly rivals – Neath!

'The boot was thrown away....'

APPENDIX 3

Matches Against Tourists (A = Aberavon; N = Neath):

October 15, 1908 – Aberavon/Neath 0 Australia 15 (at Neath).
Aust – Tries: Daniel Carroll 2, 'Paddy' Moran. Cons: Phil Carmichael 3.

September 24, 1927 – Aberavon/Neath 5 New South Wales ('Waratahs') 24 (at Aberavon).
Aberavon/Neath – Try: Dan Jones (N). Con: Jack Jeremy (A).
NSW – Tries: Cyril Towers 2, James Tancred, Ted Thorn. Cons: Tom Lawton 3. Pens: Lawton 2.

November 28, 1931 – Aberavon/Neath 3 South Africa 8 (at Neath).
Aberavon/Neath – Try: Gordon Hopkins (N).
SA – Try: Phil Mostert. Con: Bennie Osler. Pen: Osler.

December 14, 1935 – Aberavon/Neath 3 New Zealand 13 (at Aberavon).
Aberavon/Neath – Pen: Tommy Owen James (A).
NZ – Tries: Charlie Oliver, Jack Griffiths, Hugh McLean. Cons: Mike Gilbert 2.

October 28, 1939 – Aberavon/Neath v Australia (at Neath). Game cancelled. War was declared and the tourists returned home without playing a single match in GB.

March 2, 1946 – Aberavon 4 'Kiwis' (2nd NZ Expeditionary Forces) 17 (at Aberavon).
Aberavon – DG: Len Howard.
Kiwis – Tries: Jim Sherratt 2, Jim Kearney, George Nelson. Con: Bob Scott. Pen: Scott.

October 25, 1947 – Aberavon/Neath 9 Australia 19 (at the Gnoll, Neath).
Aberavon/Neath – Try: Emlyn Davies (A). Pens: Granville Jones 2 (N).
Aust – Tries: Trevor Allan, Arthur Tonkin, Cyril Burke. Cons: Brian Piper 2. Pens: Piper 2.

November 17, 1951 – Aberavon/Neath 0 South Africa 22 (at Aberavon).
SA – Tries: 'Buks' Marais 3, 'Chum' Ochse, Stephen Fry. Cons: 'Okey' Geffin 2. Pen: Geffin.

January 23, 1954 – Aberavon/Neath 5 New Zealand 11 (at Neath).
Aberavon/Neath – Try: Courtenay Meredith (N). Con: Ross Richards (A).
NZ – Tries: Ron Jarden, Stuart Freebairn. Con: Bob Scott. DG: Scott.

December 28, 1957 – Aberavon/Neath 3 Australia 5 (at Aberavon).
Aberavon/Neath – Try: D.Crowley (N).
Aust – Try: John Thornett. Con: Ray Harvey.

January 14, 1961 – Aberavon/Neath 5 South Africa 25 (at Neath).
Aberavon/Neath – Try: Tony O'Connor (A). Con: Grahame Hodgson (N).
SA – Tries: Jan Engelbrecht 2, Dave Stewart, Ian Kirkpatrick, Ron Hill,
Doug Hopwood.
Cons: 'Frik' du Preez, Dick Lockyear. Pen: du Preez.

November 17, 1963 – Aberavon/Neath 6 New Zealand 11 (at Aberavon).
Aberavon/Neath – Try: **Len Cunningham (A) (or Peter Jones {A}). Pen:
Grahame Hodgson (N).
NZ – Tries: Ian Smith, Paul Little, Ken Gray. Con: Don Clarke.
(**both claimed the try!)

October 29, 1966 – Aberavon/Neath 3 Australia 9 (at Neath).
Aberavon/Neath – Try: Dai Morris (N).
Aust – Pens: Jim Lenehan 2. DG: Lenehan.

December 10, 1969 – Aberavon/Neath 0 South Africa 27 (at Aberavon).
SA – Tries: Eben Olivier 2, Johan van der Merwe, Piet van Deventer, Renier
Grobler, Andrew van der Watt. Cons: Piet Visagie 3. Pen: Visagie.

December 15, 1973 – Aberavon/Neath 3 New Zealand 43 (at Neath).
Aberavon/Neath – Pen: Allan Martin.
NZ – Tries: Bob Burgess 2, Ian Kirkpatrick, Joe Karam, Grant Batty, Andy
Hurst, Mark Sayers.
Cons: Karam 6. Pen: Karam.

October 6, 1976 – Aberavon 6 Argentina 18 (at Aberavon).
Aberavon – Pens: John Bevan 2.
Argentine – Try: Adolfo Travaglini. Con: Gonzalo Varela. Pens: Varela 3,
Martin Sansot.

Aberavon Centenary Match.
October 19, 1976 – Aberavon 9 WRU President's XV 0 (at Aberavon).

Aberavon – Try: Clive Williams. Con: Greg Rees. Pen: Rees.

November 1, 1976 – Aberavon 13 Italy 4 (at Aberavon).
Aberavon – Tries: Steve Roper, Ogwen Alexander. Con: Allan Martin. DG: Ian Hall.
Italy – Try: F.Bessone.

November 9, 1982 – Aberavon 6 NZ Maoris 34 (at Aberavon).
Aberavon – Pens: Mike Lewis 2.
Maoris – Tries: Mike Clamp 3, Stephen Pokere 2, Warren McLean. Cons: McLean 2. Pens: McLean 2.

October 26, 1988 – Aberavon 21 Western Samoa 11 (at Aberavon).
Aberavon – Tries: John Hopkins, Neil Forester, Andrew Jones, Phil Middleton. Con: Lyndon Lewis. Pen: Lewis.
Western Samoa – Tries: Lino Foai, Lolani Koko. Pen: Tupo Faamasino.

APPENDIX 4

Rugby League:

The following turned to Rugby League in England and Wales, but though these played for Aberavon, some may not have 'Gone North' directly from the club. Also, there may be others to add to the list – who knows! In later years, some were allowed to return to play Union again:

Jack F.Avery; Arthur Bassett; Ivor Bennett; Elwyn Bowen; Kelvin Coslett; Dennis Curling; Benjamin Davies; George Davies; William Avon Davies; Alan Edwards; Thomas (Tommy) Egan; John Evans; Jim Evans; William George Evans; Robert Fleay; Howell de Francis; Arthur Edward Freear; Bernard Patrick Gould; Ossie Griffiths; Len Howard; Kevin James; Bryn James; Granville James; William Henry James; Mike Jarman; Clive Jones; David ('Tarw') Jones; Denzil ('Buck') Jones; Ike Jones; Robert (Bob) Jones; Val D. ('Bookie') Jones; Randall Lewis; Richard (Dick) Lloyd; Len Madden; Dennis Madden; Mike Nicholas; Len Oates; Ike Owens; Gwyn Parker; Tom Parker; Brin Phillips; Brian Radford; 'Buller' Rees; Francis Reynolds; Rees Richards; Johnny Ring; Gary Schofield (from RL and back); Wilfred Selby; Danny Sheehy; Kerry Sheehy; Anthony Thomas; Tommy ('Wigan') Thomas; William (Willie) Thomas; Bobby Wanbon; Fred Watkins; Ray Wilkins; W.Cliff Wilkins; Evan Williams; Max Williams and Syd Williams.

Others played at one time for Aberavon, such as Evan B. Rees, William R. ('Taffy') Davies, Mark Jones, Alan Rees, Mike Healy, Ioan Bebb, Shane McIntosh, Darren Ryan, Sean O'Brien, Daran Griffiths, Richard Lewis, Paul Morgan and David Hawkins.

Fred Perrett, a forward from Briton Ferry moved to Leeds RL in 1913. He won six Wales RU caps in 1912-13, while with Neath, but died of his wounds in France in December 1918, just after the end of World War One.

APPENDIX 5

CLUB RECORDS:

Glamorgan League Champions
1904-05

Welsh Club Champions
1923-24; 1924-25; 1925-26; 1926-27; 1960-61

Welsh Club Runners-up
1913-14; 1928-29; 1934-35; 1937-38; 1938-39; 1974-75

Welsh Challenge Cup Winners
1913-14 (beat Blaina 10-0 at Bridgend 2/5/1914)

Welsh Cup Runners-up
1973-74; 1974-75; 2010-11

WRU Cup Semi-Finalists
1971-72; 1973-74; 1974-75; 1976-77; 1977-78; 1978-79; 1981-82; 1983-84;
1986-87; 1987-88; 1989-90; 2003-04; 2004-05; 2007-08; 2008-09; 2010-
2011; 2012-13; 2014-15.

Floodlight Alliance Winners
1965-66 (beat Bridgend in final over 2 legs).

Merit Table Runners Up
1974-75; 1976-77.

Welsh League Div 1 Champions
1994-95; 1996-97*; 2000-01**; 2001-02***.

Welsh League Div 1 Runners-Up (& Promoted)
1991-92; 1997-98****; 2002-03.

Premiership Runners-up
2016-17.

* WRU changed rules mid-season – Aberavon not promoted.
** WRU changed rules a week before start of season – Aberavon not promoted.
*** Lost two-leg play-off v Premier Division side Caerphilly – Aberavon
not promoted.
**** WRU promoted Aberavon 4 days before 1998-99 season due to Cardiff
   & Swansea dropping out.

Record Win
114-10 v Glyncorrwg (a) 31/8/2003.

Record Win (League)
102-5 v Caerphilly (h) 1/5/2004.

Record Win (Cup)
93-0 v Abertillery (h) 21/12/2002.

Heaviest Defeat (Cup)
13-97 v Montferrand (a) (European Shield) 7/10/1998.

Heaviest Defeat (League)
17-95 v Neath (a) 3/4/1996.

Most Capped Player
Allan Martin 34 (1973-81).

Most Points in a Season
1643 (2002-03).

Most League Points in a Season
1260 (2002-03).

Most Tries in a Season
222 (2002-03).

Most League Tries in a Season
161 (2002-03).

Highest Points Scorer in a Season
515 Jamie Davies (2002-03).

Highest League Points Scorer in a Season
451 Jamie Davies (2002-03).

Over 1,000 Points in a Career
4,130 Jamie Davies (1996 & 2000-14)
1,572 Mike Lewis (1980-88)
1,208 Tommy Owen James (1927-46)
1,181 Allan Martin (1968-89)
1,045 Ross Richards (1948-60).

Most Points in a Game
38 Greg Rees v Barbados 1977 (a);
33 Jamie Davies (3t, 6c, 2p) v British Steel (h)(Central Glamorgan Cup)
   31/1/2001.

Most Points in a Game (League)
32 Jamie Davies (2t, 11c) v Caerphilly (h) 1/5/2004.

Most Games Won Consecutively
19 – 2001-02 (all games)
20 – 2001-02 (League only)
29 – home league games 2001-03

Highest Try Scorer Pre War
125 Johnny Ring (1919-20 to 1921-22)
122 Charlie Rowlands
119 Jack Thomas (1931-46)

Highest Try Scorer Post War
163 Richard Carter
155 Richard Morris
128 Daran Griffiths
122 John Collins
119 John Evans
106 Ken Thomas
101 Jamie Davies & Les Keen
100 Peter Jones

Most Tries in a Season (Pre War)
46 Johnny Ring (1921-22).

Most Tries in a Season (Post War)
28 Dennis Curling (1971-72); Lee Abdul (2002-03).

Most Tries in a Season by a Forward
25 Richard Morris (2002-03).

Most League Tries in a Season
25 Sam Greenaway (2001-02).

Most Tries in a Game
7 Johnny Ring (1921-22)
7 Dennis Curling (v Nantymoel, Cup 17/11/71).

Most Tries in a Game (League)
4 Lee Abdul; Sam Greenaway.

Most league points (Career)
3,261 Jamie Davies (1996 & 2000-14).

Scores of 100 and over
114-10 v Glyncorrwg (a-31/8/2003)

110-0 v Dinas Powys (a-14/9/2007)
108-0 v Chepstow (a-10/8/2002)
102-0 v 7th Parachute Regiment (h-22/3/2002)
102-5 v Caerphilly (League) (h-1/5/2004).

Biggest Welsh Cup loss
3-72 v Cardiff (a) (8/4/1995).

Most appearances
540 Richard Morris

(NB: those of Billy Mainwaring and Allan Martin were no doubt higher, though they were never fully recorded)

APPENDIX 6

Aberavon's International Players (capped while playing for the club)

1 – DANiel Jones. Caps: 1. Scrum half. 1897 v E (try).
   Born: 31/5/1875 Taibach. Died: 1/1/1959 Taibach.

2 – Alfred Bailey ('BOBBY') Brice. Caps: 18. Forward.
   1899 v E,S,I; 1900 v E,S,I; 1901 v E.S.I; 1902 v E,S,I (con); 1903 v E,S,I (try); 1904 v E,S (try),I.
   Born: 23/9/1871 Weare, Somerset. Died: 28/5/1938 Port Talbot. (15 caps at Aberavon/3 at Cardiff).

3 – John Josiah ('BALA') Jones. Caps: 1. Scrum half. 1901 v E.
   Born: Jan-March 1875 Aberavon. Died: Jan-March 1959 Neath.

4 – GEORGE Vickery. CAP FOR ENGLAND. Caps: 1. Forward. England v Ireland 1905.
   Born: 25/5/1879 Chard, Somerset. Died: July 1970 Neath. (Father of Walter).

5 – William Avon (WILLIE) Davies. Caps: 2. Centre. 1912 v S,I.
   Born: 27/12/1890 Aberavon. Died: 18/9/1967 Exeter. RL: Leeds/Wales/GB.

6 – REES Richards. Caps: 3. Forward. 1913 v S,F,I.
   Born: 3/5/1886 Cwmavon. Died: 29/6/1953 Neath. RL: Wigan/Wales.

7 – James (JIM) Jones. Caps: 6. Forward. 1919 v NZ Army; 1920 v E,S; 1921 v S,F,I.
   Born: 4th qtr 1893 Blaengwynfai, Port Talbot. Died: 3/3/1934 Briton Ferry.

8 – John (JOHNNY) Ring. Caps: 1. Wing. 1921 v E (try).
   Born: 14/11/1900 Port Talbot. Died: 10/11/1984 Wigan. RL:Wigan/Rochdale/Wales/GB. Wigan RL – 368 tries in 329 games; GB RL to Aust/NZ 1924 – 23 tries in 15 games.

9 – John Llewellyn (LLEW) Jenkins. Caps: 2. Forward. 1923 v S,F.
   Born: 12/3/1903 Maesteg. Died: 4/7/1973 Coventry.

10 – JOHN Henry Davies. Caps: 1. Forward. 1923 v I.
   Born: c.1897. Died: 1940s Port Talbot. Killed in accident involving two buses.

11 – David Henry ('HUNT') Davies. Caps: 1. Centre. 1924 v E.
   Born: 11/11/1896 Pott Talbot. Died: 8/5/1979 Cimla.
   Lost part of a foot in WW1 and played with a reinforced boot.

12 – Robert John (BOB) Randall. Caps: 2. Forward. 1924 v I,F.

Born: 11/12/1890 Neath. Died: 7/7/1965 Port Talbot.

13 – William John (WILLIE) Hopkins. Caps: 2. Fly half. 1925 v E,S.
Born: 18/6/1896 Aberavon. Died: 7/7/1968 Nefyn, Pwllheli.

14 – William Henry (WILLIE) James. Caps: 2. Wing. 1925 v E (try),S.
Born: 16/7/1902 Aberavon. Died: 27/2/1972 Aberavon. (Brother of Tommy). RL: Leeds/Carlisle/Acton & Willesden/Streatham & Mitcham/Castleford/Newcastle.

15 – Brinley (BRIN) Phillips. Caps: 5. Forward. 1925 v E,S,F,I; 1926 v E.
Born: 11/10/1900 Merthyr. Died: April-June 1980 Neath. RL: Huddersfield/Wales.

16 – EVAN Williams. Caps: 2. Centre. 1925 v E,S.
Born: 18/6/1906 Port Talbot. Died: 18/11/1976 Leeds. RL: Leeds/Hunslet.

17 – Charles Foster (CHARLIE) Rowlands. Caps: 1. Wing. 1926 v I.
Born: July-Sept 1899 Merthyr. Died: 10/11/1958 Morriston.

18 – Edward McDonald ('NED') Jenkins. Caps: 21. Forward.
1927 v S,F,I,NSW; 1928 v E,S,I,F; 1929 v F; 1930 v E,S,I,F; 1931 v E,S,F,I,SA; 1932 v E,S,I.
Born: 28/7/1904 Tonyrefail. Died: 8/11/1990 Porthcawl.

19 – Charles Albert ('TAL') Harris. Caps: 1. Scrum half. 1927 v NSW.
Born: 4/2/1902 Maindy, Cardiff. Died: 1/10/1963 Aberavon.

20 – ARTHUR Bassett. Caps: 6. Wing. 1934 v I; 1935 v E,S,I; 1938 v E,S.
Born: 28/6/1914 Kenfig Hill. Died: 30/12/1999 Matlock, Derbyshire.
RL: Halifax/York/Wales/GB (to Aust/NZ 1946).

21 – Thomas Owen (TOMMY) James. Caps: 2. Full back. 1935 v I (pen); 1937 v S.
Born: 6/10/1904 Aberavon. Died: 8/4/1984 Port Talbot. (Brother of Willie James).

22 – Griffith Morgan (GRIFF) Williams. Caps: 3. Forward. 1936 v E,S,I.
Born: 30/6/1907 Pontypridd. Died: April 1991 Neath.

23 – IVOR Bennett. Caps: 1. Prop. 1937 v I.
Born: 16/6/1913 Aberkenfig. Died: 16/6/2003 Neath/Port Talbot Hospital. RL: Warrington/Bridgend.

24 – WALTER Elias Vickery. Caps: 4. Forward. 1938 v E,S,I; 1939 v E.
Born: 25/10/1909 Port Talbot. Died: 7/4/2000 Neath Hospital. (Son of George).

25 – SYDney Arthur Williams. Caps: 3. Wing. 1939 v E,S,I.
Born: 17/4/1918 Aberavon. Died: 28/8/1976 Neath. 7 Services caps.
RL: Salford/Wales. First Aberavon player for the Barbarians – 4 try-debut v East Midlands 1939.

26 – EMLYN Price Davies. Caps: 2. Prop. 1947 A; 1948 I.

Born: 15/1/1922 Port Talbot. Died: 6/9/2016 Cymmer.
In June 2014 he had became the oldest living Welsh international.

27 – David GLYNdwr John. Caps: 2. Centre/Fly half. 1954 v E,F.
Born: 22/2/1932 Neath. Died: 7/6/1983 Bridgend.

28 – RORY O'Connor. Caps: 1. Blind-side wing forward. 1957 v E.
Born: 14/9/1932 Neath. Died: 7/3/1986 Neath.

29 – JOHN Ernest Collins. Caps: 10. Wing.
1958 v A (try),E,S (try),F (try); 1959 v E,S,I,F; 1960 v E; 1961 v F.
Born: 16/1/1931 Aberavon. Died: 9/5/2017 Port Talbot.

30 – CLIFFord Ashton. Caps: 7. Fly half. 1959 v E,S,I; 1960 v E,S,I; 1962 v I.
Born: 17/12/1932 Cwmavon. Died: 29/3/2001 Newport.

31 – HAYDN John Davies. Caps: 2. Centre. 1959 v E,S.
Born: 21/11/1936 Cowbridge. Cambridge University.

32 – Leonard John (LEN) Cunningham. Caps: 14. Prop. 1960 v E,S,I,F; 1962 v E,S,F,I; 1963 v NZ; 1964 v E,S,I,F,SA.
Born: 3/1/1931 Port Talbot. Died: 20/7/1998 Bridgend.

33 – Anthony (TONY) O'Connor. Caps: 5. Scrum half. 1960 v SA; 1961 v E,S; 1962 v F,I.
Born: 24/4/1934 Neath. Died: 22/5/2015 Porthcawl. Oxford University. Lions 1962.

34 – PHILip Edward John Morgan. Caps: 3. Prop. 1961 v E,S,F.
Born: 21/12/1937 Hereford. Died: 9/4/1998 Kenfig Hill.

35 – DAVID Lynn Thomas. Caps: 1. Centre. 1961 v I.
Born: 29/4/1941 Pontrhydyfen. Died: 3/1/2017 Porthcawl.

36 – Thomas KELvin Coslett. Caps: 3. Full back. 1962 v E,S,F.
Born: 14/1/1942 Bynea. RL: St Helen's (3,413 pts in 531 games)/ Rochdale/Wales.

37 – ROGER Carl Brandon Michaelson. Caps: 1. No 8. 1963 v E.
Born: 31/3/1941 Porthcawl. Cambridge University.

38 – Gwilym Thomas (BILLY) Mainwaring. Caps: 6. Lock. 1967 v S,I,F,E,NZ; 1968 v E.
Born: 24/1/1941 Port Talbot. Now officially William Thomas Mainwaring.

39 – IAN Hall. Caps: 8. Centre/Wing. 1967 v NZ; 1970 v SA,S,E; 1971 v S; 1974 v S,I,F.
Born: 4/11/1946 Gilfach Goch.

40 – PAUL James Wheeler. Caps: 2. Full back. 1967 v NZ; 1968 v E.
Born: 5/2/1947 Newport.

41 – MAXwell Lloyd Wiltshire. Caps: 4. Lock. 1967 v NZ; 1968 v E,S,F.
Born: 16/7/1938 Milsom Point, Sydney, Australia.

42 – Robert (BOBBY) Wanbon. Caps: 1. No 8. 1968 v E (try).

Born: 16/11/1943 Port Talbot. RL: St Helen's/Warrington/Wales.

43 – ALLAN Jeffrey Martin. Caps: 34. Lock. 1973 v A; 1974 v S,I; 1975
v F,E,S,I,A; 1976 v E,S,I,F; 1977 v I,F,E,S; 1978 v E,S,I,F,A(1)(2),NZ;
1979 v S,I,F,E; 1980 v F,E,S,I,NZ; 1981 v I,F.
(1t, 3c, 5p). Lions 1977 & 1980. Born: 11/12/1948 Port Talbot.

44 – Robert CLIVE Shell. Caps: 1. (Rep) Scrum half. 1973 v A(r).
Born: 9/9/1947 Pyle. Died: 6/1/2012 Pyle.

45 – JOHN David Bevan. Caps: 4. Fly half. 1975 v F,E,S,A.
Born: 12/3/1948 Neath. Died: 5/6/1986 Port Talbot. Lions 1977. Wales
coach 1982-85.

46 – CLIVE Williams. Caps: 8. Prop. 1977 v E,S; 1980 v F,E,S,I,NZ; 1983 v
E.
Born: 2/11/1948 Porthcawl. (2 caps at Aberavon/6 at Swansea). Lions
1977 & 1980.

47 – Stanley JOHN Richardson. Caps: 2. Prop. 1978 v A(2,r); 1979 v E.
Born: 1/4/1947 Blaencwm, near Treherbert.

48 – LESlie Keen. Caps: 4. Wing. 1980 v F,E,S (try),I.
Born: 13/11/1954 Port Talbot.

49 – William John (BILLY) James. Caps: 21. Hooker. 1983 v E,S,I,F,Rom;
1984 v S; 1985 v S,I,F,E,Fiji (try); 1986 v E,S,I,F,Fiji,Ton,WSam; 1987
v E,S,I.
Born: 18/7/1956 Port Talbot. Only Aberavon player to captain Wales
(v Ireland 1987).

50 – RAYmond Giles. Caps: 3. Scrum half. 1983 v Rom; 1985 v Fiji(r); 1987
v Can(WC).
Born: 15/1/1961 Kenfig Hill.

51 – TIMothy John Fauvel. Caps: 1. (Rep) No 8. 1988 v NZ(1,r).
Born: 9/6/1960 Bridgend.

APPENDIX 7

Unsung Hero – Steve Jones

No history of Aberavon could be complete without mentioning Steve Jones.

The man who never comes to club dinners, awards, etc and is never in the squad photograph. The man who is almost taken for granted by players and supporters. The man who is always there on match days, training nights and probably most days of the week.

Clubs praise Aberavon RFC for the condition of the pitch – that is because of Steve, the groundsman. The players all get there on time – that is because of Steve, the team manager.

When Simon King was starting as club coach he asked me what this bloke Jones was like. I could only reply that you would not find a more loyal man. Loyal to the coach; loyal to the chairman; loyal to the players and loyal to the club as a whole. Loyal, even if, for example, he deep down sometimes disagreed with selection.

He doesn't want praise so this is as near to it that he is getting!!

Thanks Steve from all of us and congratulations on winning the WRU's 'Unsung Hero' Award in May 2017.

APPENDIX 8

Other Significant Games Hosted at the Talbot Athletic Ground included:

Internationals

1951 – Wales Secondary Schools 6 Wales Youth 3.
1958 – Wales Under-15s 28 South of Scotland 0.
1968 – Wales Secondary Schools 5 Yorkshire 3.
1976 – Wales Secondary Schools 26 Ireland 10.
1978 – Wales B 18 France B 31. (Jeff Griffiths (Aberavon) scored the only Wales try. Serge Blanco (France) scored 19 points.)
1979 – Glamorgan 22 Carmarthenshire 4 (Welsh Counties Final).
1982 – Wales Youth 17 England Colts 27.
1989 – Wales Youth 9 France 17.
1992 – Wales Districts 10 Holland 25.
1994 – Wales Secondary Schools 35 Scotland 8.
1995 – Wales Schools und-18s 21 Japan 18.
1996 – Wales Youth 34 Italy 8; Wales Students 15 France 41.
2004 – Wales under-19s 21 Scotland 12.
2005 – Wales under-16s 10 England 24; Wales under-16s A v England A.
2006 – Wales under-18s 19 France 24; Wales under-19s 48 Scotland 10.
2006 – Wales under-19s 32 Italy 18; Wales under-19s 32 France 12.
2006 – Premiership Play-off – Maesteg 19 Bonymaen 6.
2007 – Wales under-19s v England (postponed – rain); Welsh Colleges 44 England 7.
2008 – Wales under-18s 24 Scotland 0.
2009 – Wales under-18s 29 Italy 6.
2013 – Wales Women 10 Ireland 12; Wales Women 16 England 20.
2014 – Wales Women 11 Italy 12; Wales Women 0 France 27.
2014 – Wales Women 25 Scotland 0.
2015 – Silver Ball Final – Penallta 22 Ystrad Rhondda 17.
2016 – Silver Ball Final – Bedlinog 32 Porth Quins 15.
2016 – Wales Women 12 Italy 16.

Welsh Cup Semi-Finals

1973 – Cardiff 12 Swansea 8
1974 – Llanelli 16 Pontypool 14

1978 – Swansea 18 Cardiff 13
1983 – Pontypool 16 Bridgend 3
2006 – Neath 50 Maesteg 9
2007 – Llandovery 20 Llanelli 19
2008 – Neath 49 Glamorgan Wanderers 37
2013 – Pontypridd 18 Carmarthen Quins 16
2015 – Bridgend 22 Carmarthen Quins 20
2016 – Carmarthen Quins 21 Cross Keys 20
2017 – Pontypridd 42 Cross Keys 37

Fosters Cup Semi-Final

2017 – Carmarthen Quins 37 Merthyr 31

The Talbot Athletic Ground down the years.

St David's Press

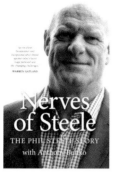

NERVES OF STEELE
The Phil Steele Story

'I've been lucky enough to get to know Phil during my time as Wales coach. He is an excellent broadcaster who genuinely wants Wales and Welsh players to excel and I respect his friendly and personal approach. I also admire the fact that he has been able to do this while facing personal and life changing challenges.'
Warren Gatland

'Phil Steele embodies all that is great about the culture of Welsh rugby. His strength of character and sense of fun are all the more impressive given some of the dark and devastating times he has endured.' **Caroline Hitt**

Known to thousands of rugby fans as a knowledgeable, passionate and witty broadcaster, and as an entertaining and popular after-dinner speaker, Phil Steele's confident demeanour and humorous disposition mask a life-long battle against depression and anxiety heightened by heartbreak and tragedy in his personal life. Nerves of Steele is a remarkable story and reveals the real Phil Steele, a man known only by his very closest friends and family.

978-1-902719-50-4   208pp   £13.99   PB
978-1-902719-53-5   £9.99 eBook

2 HARD TO HANDLE
The Autobiography of Mike 'Spikey' Watkins

'One of the most inspirational leaders that Welsh rugby has ever produced'
Mike Ruddock

'A great friend...also a great inspiration...he led from the front and his team mates could always rely on him when things got a bit rough, even though he'd probably started it!!' **Paul Turner**

'No one trained harder, no one played harder...heart of a lion' **Terry Holmes**

One of the most colourful and controversial characters in Welsh rugby history, Mike 'Spikey' Watkins remains the only player since 1882 to captain Wales on his debut, and win.

978-1-902719-40-5   251pp   £18.99   PB

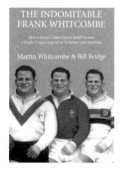

THE INDOMITABLE FRANK WHITCOMBE
How a Genial Giant from Cardiff became a Rugby League Legend in Yorkshire and Australia

'Frank Whitcombe was a rugby league cult hero in the days before there were cult heroes. An eighteen-stone battle tank of a prop forward, he graduated from Welsh rugby union to become a pillar of the great Bradford pack of the 1940s. In the process, he became the first forward to win the Lance Todd Trophy, a member of the 1946 'itable' Lions touring team to Australasia and had even driven the team bus to Wembley when Bradford won the 1947 Challenge Cup Final. This book is his story - it is essential reading for anyone interested in the history of rugby and the amazing men who made the game.' **Prof. Tony Collins**

'Frank Whitcombe became a Welsh international and a Great Britain tourist. He is widely regarded as an all-time great of rugby league.' **Fran Cotton**

978-1-902719-47-4   256pp   £19.99   PB
978-1-902719-59-7   £9.99   eBook

ST DAVID'S PRESS

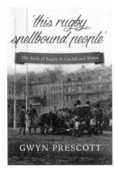

'THIS RUGBY SPELLBOUND PEOPLE'
The Birth of Rugby in Cardiff and Wales

"...scrupulously researched [and] well written...Gwyn Prescott has given [rugby in Wales] a history to be proud of." **Huw Richards, scrum.com**

"Prescott paints a meticulous picture of Welsh rugby's growth in Victorian Britain" **Rugby World**

"...a fascinating piece of research and a major contribution to the history of rugby." **Tony Collins**

The Birth of Rugby in Cardiff and Wales is the essential guide to the importance of rugby in Cardiff and to the significance of Cardiff to the development of Welsh rugby in the nineteenth century.

978-1-902719-43-6   304pp   £16.99   PB

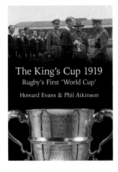

THE KING'S CUP 1919
Rugby's First World Cup

'An intriguing retelling of a significant but largely forgotten chapter of rugby union history, superbly illustrated.' **Huw Richards**

'Howard is an authority on rugby's history and meticulous in his research' **Andy Howell, Western Mail**

The world of rugby celebrated the 8th Rugby World Cup in 2015, but a tournament held in 1919, The King's Cup, can rightly claim to be rugby's first competitive 'World Cup'.

Meticulously compiled by Howard Evans and Phil Atkinson, The King's Cup 1919 is the first book to tell the full story of rugby's first 'World Cup' and is essential reading for all rugby enthusiasts and military historians.

978-1-902719-44-3   192pp   £14.99   PB

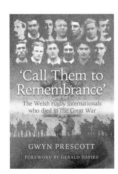

'CALL THEM TO REMEMBRANCE'
The Welsh Rugby Internationals who died in the Great War

This book is [an] acknowledgment of the sacrifice made by 13 Welshmen....Theirs was a sacrifice which needs to be told....Gwyn Prescott, with meticulous and sympathetic attention to detail, tells the story. This narrative is an essential record'. **Gerald Davies**

'These humbling stories describe thirteen individual journeys which began on muddy yet familiar Welsh playing fields but ended in the unimaginable brutality of the battles of the First World War.' www.gwladrugby.com

'Call them to remembrance', which includes 120 illustrations and maps, tells the stories of thirteen Welsh heroes who shared the common bond of having worn the famous red jersey of the Welsh international rugby team.

978-1-902719-37-5   170pp   £14.99   PB